NEEDLEPOINT

Mrs. Ward Briggs of Montchanin, Delaware adapted an illustration from an issue of *Ducks Unlimited* for the design of the Canada Geese. To achieve the tweedy effect she combined two different colors in her needle.

NEEDLEPOINT

Revised and Enlarged

HOPE HANLEY

Charles Scribner's Sons / New York

18th century English fans on page i reproduced by *courtesy of The Metropolitan Museum of Art, collection of Irwin Untermyer.*

Photographs: T. J. Healy II, page ii, W. Churcher, page 2; Lee Salsbery, pages 8, 10, 14, 16, 19, 23, 27, 32, 40, 151, 152, 159, 160, 161, Plate 14; Bob Burchette, page 13; Hans Nes Studio, page 135, Plate 1; Sussman and Ochs, page 136; Helga Studio, Plates 4, 7, 9, 17; Richard A. Little, Plate 8; Hugh Grubb, pages 71, 99, Plate 15; all others by Allen Bress.

Greeting card on page 32 reprinted by kind permission of Hallmark Cards Inc.

This book published simultaneously in the
United States of America and in Canada—
Copyright under the Berne Convention

1 3 5 7 9 11 13 15 17 19 C/MD 20 18 16 14 12 10 8 6 4 2

Printed in the United States of America
Library of Congress Catalog Card Number 74-14016
ISBN 0-684-140365

Books by Hope Hanley

Needlepoint
New Methods in Needlepoint
Needlepoint in America
Needlepoint Rugs
Fun with Needlepoint
The ABCs of Needlepoint

Acknowledgements

Having the opportunity to revise one's own book is like having the chance to live your life over again. I hope I can set things "straight" this time, my thanks to Elinor Parker for the chance to do so. My gratitude goes to Lewis Rockwell of New York for finding me such lovely new examples of needlepoint to photograph as well as to Mrs. Philip Weymouth of Delaware, Mrs. Richard Rheutan of Florida, and Mrs. Billie Conkling of Baltimore. My thanks also to the kind people who permitted me to use their work. I wish to thank Doris Bowman of the Smithsonian Institution and James M. O'Neill of the District of Columbia Public Library for the second time for their help when I first wrote this book.

CONTENTS

Introduction   1

Canvas   3

Wool   11

Frames   17

Design   21

The Stitches   37

Ways of Joining Canvas   137

Finishing Your Canvas   145

Et Cetera   155

Rugs   163

Bibliography   167

Index of Stitches   169

Notes   173

COLOR PLATES

following page 80 and page 144

1   Pole Screen
2   Needlepoint Picture
3   Kneeler
4   Rug
5   Wall Hanging
6   Berlin Work Picture
7   Bargello Rug
8   Bargello Wall Hanging
9   Needlepoint Fan
10 Needlepoint Rug
11 Raised Work Picture
12 Needlepoint Bag
13 Reverse Side of Bag
14 Sampler
15 Evolution Hanging
16 Op Art Picture
17 Sampler Tote Bag
18 Christmas Stocking

The King Charles Spaniel with his bright eyes is worked in the surrey stitch, c. 1870. The contours of his body were skillfully clipped in. The dog sits on a silk cross stitch cushion with beaded trim. *The Smithsonian Institution, Washington, D.C.*

NEEDLEPOINT

A chair in the Governor's Palace, Williamsburg, upholstered in petit point in a lightly colored floral design. *Colonial Williamsburg.*

INTRODUCTION

What is needlepoint? Needlepoint is counted embroidery stitches worked with a needle over the threads of a canvas. There are basically only two kinds of needlepoint stitches: short stitches covering one mesh or thread, and long stitches covering two or more mesh or threads. These two basic stitches can be handled in two different ways to form more variations. The long or the short stitches may either be "tied down" or cross themselves in some way. All needlepoint stitches trace their origin back to the two basic stitches, or one or both of the variations.

This book is intended for the person who wants to do more than just fill in backgrounds of needlepoint canvases with the half cross stitch. It is intended for the person who wants to create something original, for the person who wants to use needlepoint as his personal art medium. In this book you will find designing techniques which apply to needlepoint. There are over eighty needlepoint stitches here for you to try. Experiment with them, combine them. Mix them as *you* please.

The beginning needlepointer will perhaps be hesitant to jump right in and start designing. An easy way to get the feel of "painting" with wool and to touch on the fringes of designing is to buy a professionally designed canvas which will come complete with the right amount of wool. There are also on the market some very attractive canvases with part of the design worked and the rest traméed as a design guide for the buyer. A canvas with the design already completed would be the most economical procedure for the person who just wants to experiment with new background stitches. Any of the above suggestions will surely spark some designing ideas and you will have your first canvas designed (mentally, anyway) before you have completed your experimental piece.

To many needlepointers much of the material in this book will not be new, but perhaps it will serve as a reminder of stitches forgotten or techniques untried.

Some of the stitches in this book date back to the time of Mary, Queen of Scots. One or two were gleaned from stitchery books of a hundred years ago. The Metropolitan Museum in New York is the best source for seeing how the old stitches were once used. The National Cathedral (the seat of the Presiding Bishop of the Protestant Episcopal Church of the United States) in Washington, D. C. is the best place to see how needlepoint stitches and design can be used today. But don't stick to what others have done. *Experiment!* This book will show you the techniques and then you are on your own to create as you will.

CANVAS

Types of Canvas and Their Uses

Mono-Canvas   There are three basic weaves of canvas, mono-canvas, penelope or two thread, and leno canvas. Mono canvas or "uni" as it is sometimes called is a single thread or plain weave canvas. The warp thread is placed an even distance away from the weft thread. Mono-canvas is made of a slightly heavier thread than the other canvases, and has a polished look which is due to the sizing. The purpose of the sizing is to keep the threads in place and separated while it is being woven and then worked. Mono-canvas is very easy to paint on because of the heavy sizing; it is also very easy on the eyes because of the simple weave. It is usually white in color although it can be had in a tannish color called ecru, and a fine eighteen mesh canvas is peach in color. It is available from ten mesh to the inch to twenty-four mesh to the inch. All canvas is described by the number of mesh or threads per inch. Mono-canvas is used for gros point, petit point and bargello or any of the upright stitches.

Mono-canvas does not have a very even mesh count. This means that if you measure off seven inches of mono-canvas in each direction you would expect to count seventy mesh if the canvas is ten mesh

3

A kneeler of modern workmanship, in Chelsea Old Church, London: the design was adapted from Elizabethan embroideries in the Victoria and Albert Museum. *Courtesy, Chelsea Old Church, London.*

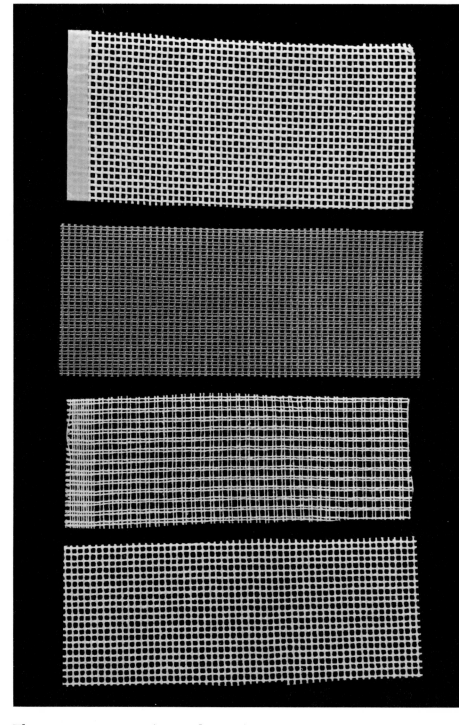

The various canvases: (top to bottom) mono canvas, penelope, two thread canvas, and leno canvas.

to the inch. The actual count will be close to seventy on the warp threads but can vary four or five mesh more or less than seventy on the weft threads. This is significant if you are working a design from a graph because of the distortion it could create in the finished canvas.

Penelope or Two-Thread Canvas There are two kinds of penelope or two-thread canvas. Both have two threads in the warp and the weft to work over, but one, penelope, has the warp threads woven very close together, and the other has the warp and weft threads an even space apart. Penelope is usually ecru in color and is made of a slightly lighter weight thread than mono-canvas. The advantage of using penelope is that you may separate the pairs of threads with your needle and make a mono-canvas of it. Thus a ten mesh penelope can be used as a twenty mesh mono-canvas all on the same project. This way details could be done in twenty mesh and the background in ten mesh. Ten/twenty is the most commonly used mesh in penelope but it can be had in twelve/twenty-four and a very durable seven/fourteen.

The two-thread canvas (with the evenly spaced threads) usually comes in white. It is not as easy to paint upon and the price is lower per yard. Two-thread canvas is available from four mesh per inch which is suitable for rugs up to sixteen mesh per inch.

Leno Canvas The newest addition to the canvas market, leno canvas is also known as interlock canvas. It is made of a thinner thread than the other canvases and is more intricately woven. Unless you look at it closely it looks like mono-canvas. Then you will see that it is a two-thread canvas with both warp and weft pairs woven very tightly together, the warp threads taking a half twist between each set of weft threads. Leno canvas is the only canvas that all needlepoint stitches can be worked on. Because the threads of leno are so close together it is possible to work upright stitches on it; and since it is a two-thread canvas, stitches that cannot be worked on loosely woven mono-canvas can be worked on leno.

Leno canvas has a very even mesh count in both directions which makes it a good canvas for graph work. It is easy to paint upon and good for silk screen and stenciling. It is available from six mesh per inch to sixteen. Needlepoint stitches can be worked on other fabrics such as Aida cloth or warp cloth. It is important that the fabric be woven evenly.

Needlepoint canvas comes in rolls forty inches wide, though it can be had as narrow as twenty-four inches or as wide as fifty-four inches. There is very little canvas made in the United States at present; most of it comes from Germany or France. It is made of cotton, of multiple threads spun into one strong thread. When buying canvas, try to avoid getting a piece with knots in it, but if it is inevitable, (warp threads do break and must be knotted) there is a remedy. Ravel off a thread from the cut edge. Unweave the offending thread and reweave with your ravelled piece.

If your project must be very durable perhaps mono-canvas or penelope would be the best to use. If you plan to join two pieces of canvas together for a rug or wall hanging, be certain that you buy all your canvas for that project from the same bolt of canvas. Because of the variation of the weave in each roll of canvas you could come up with an uneven count at the join. When cutting canvas for a pieced rug, be sure it is cut as it will lie on the floor, all warps going in the same direction. This is one reason why it is always a good idea to work your needlepoint with the selvedge on the left side, thus insuring that the warps will always be going in the same direction. To keep canvas from ravelling as you work it, bind the edges with cotton binding tape or cover with masking tape or paint with liquid latex such as Rug-Sta or Spee Dee. A cotton sewing thread basted up the center of the canvas will aid you in any counting of threads and will help you center your design. Always cut canvas evenly between two threads. If you must mark a piece of canvas, for measuring, for instance, use a dressmakers' chalk or a wax crayon. Allow a two-inch border of bare canvas around your design. You will need this when it comes time to block it.

Detail of curtains worked with Chinoiserie subjects. French, early 18th century. *The Metropolitan Museum of Art, gift of Irwin Untermyer, 1953.*

The petit point box is called a toilet cabinet. The lid lifts up to show fitted bottles and boxes. The open door reveals several little drawers. The very fine petit point was done in silk in the second half of the seventeenth century in England. *Courtesy, Mrs. George Maurice Morris.*

Gros Point and Petit Point

The only difference between gros point and petit point is the number of mesh per inch on the canvas on which they are done. A casual rule could be that any canvas with sixteen mesh per inch or *more* is petit point canvas, and any canvas over that up to say eight mesh per inch is gros point canvas. There is no special gros point stitch as such. The continental stitch is done on gros point canvas as well as petit point canvas and does not change its name according to the size mesh of the canvas.

What Needle for What Canvas?

Needles vary in size from the smallest, a size 24, by even numbers up to the largest, a size 14. These are the sizes commonly available today. Needlepoint needles are called tapestry needles and the best ones come from England. They come six to a package and are large-eyed and blunt. An easy way to remember whether a needle is large or small just by the number is to keep in mind that a low number needle is used on a low number of mesh canvas, and a high number needle is used on a high number of mesh canvas. A large yarn needle is used on low mesh rug canvas.

The needle size is proper if the canvas threads are not moved when the threaded needle is stabbed through the canvas. To give you an idea of what size needle to use on what size canvas, a size 18 needle would do well on ten mesh mono-canvas, a size 22 would do for eighteen mesh mono-canvas. Plastic pill bottles make fine needle cases.

Nelly Custis Lewis worked the firescreen which stands in the music room of her former home, Woodlawn Plantation, Mount Vernon, Virginia. The floral design was worked over canvas which was basted to wool broadcloth. Each stitch went through both canvas and cloth, upon completion the canvas threads were pulled out leaving the stitches on the broadcloth background. *The National Trust for Historic Preservation.*

WOOL

XXXXXXXXXXXXXXXXXXXX
XXXXXXXXXXXXXXXXXXX

Types of Wool Required for Different Canvases

Needlepoint wool must have long smooth fibers, therefore knitting wool is not appropriate because it has shorter, more wiry fibers.

Crewel Wool Crewel wool is used primarily for crewel embroidery but it also makes an excellent needlepoint yarn. It is a springy two-ply wool, sold in skeins or by the strand. One would use as many strands as needed to cover the canvas effectively, perhaps as many as seven or eight.

Persian Wool Persian wool is also a two-ply wool, but it is not as springy as crewel. It is sold in three thread strands which may be worked separately or all three threads at once. Thus it is a very versatile wool in that it can be used for everything from "large" petit point to "small" rug canvas. It is convenient and economical to buy because it can be bought in small quantities, some stores even sell it by the strand! For this reason it is excellent for pictorial work, one may need only one thread of a color and it is a pity to pay the price of a whole 20 yard skein just for that one thread. Most professional designers sell this wool to go with their designs and include just the right amount you need to complete the design.

When this book was first written there was just one brand of Persian wool, now there are several. They are all three-thread strands, but some of them are slightly heavier or thinner per thread than the others. Because of this variation it is not a good idea to mix brands on the same canvas. The variation also makes it impossible to recommend how much wool to use for the different mesh canvases. Do a test swatch of the wool of your choice, adding a thread if it does not seem to cover the canvas. That is the most important thing, to cover the canvas adequately. If the wool is too thick for the canvas it will push or spread the mesh and then you must subtract a strand.

Tapestry Wool   Tapestry wool is the kind sold by the department stores to finish the backgrounds of the canvases they sell. It is moth-proofed and comes in matched dye lots. It is four ply, and comes in 40 yard skeins. Needlework stores which carry Persian wool usually carry tapestry wool also.

Rug Wool   There are also many more rug yarns on the market now than there were ten years ago. They are made of real wool and synthetic fibers. Real wool will wear longer though it does cost more. If you are going to put a lot of time and effort into a rug, why not use the best materials? Rug wool may be defined as any wool that can be used single strand on a canvas seven mesh to the inch or lower. Most shops sell it by the quarter pound, a few sell it by the strand.

Silk and Cotton   Both silk and cotton are multi-thread, either four or six to the strand. They are used for highlighting, for petit point, and for outlining to give emphasis to certain parts of the design. Cotton floss does not cost very much, silk is quite expensive. The colors available in the silk are more delicate and wider in the range than the cotton. If you find the silk difficult to work with, run each strand over a block of sewing wax. It will not harm the silk or the canvas.

Raffia, chenille or rayon novelty yarns may be used but should be limited to special effects. Test them carefully for color fastness

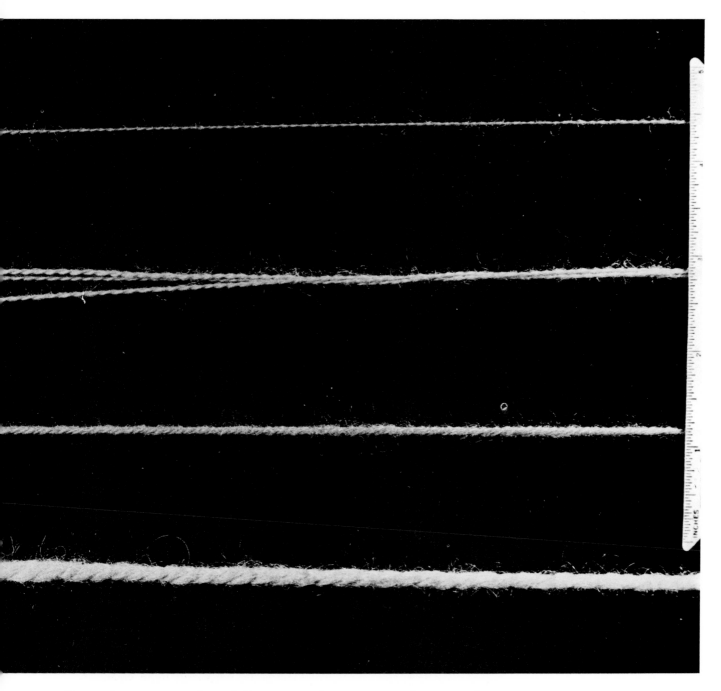

Top to bottom; crewel wool, Persian wool, tapestry wool, rug wool.

Two kneelers from the Bethlehem Chapel. The background color of all the kneelers in the chapel is dark red. *The National Cathedral, Washington, D.C.*

before using them. Wet them and lay them on a paper towel for an hour or so to see if they run. This is a good practice to follow with any yarns, even the best occasionally run.

Thrums   Though not sold in the United States, thrums are mentioned in British needlework books. They are ends of wool left over from carpet-making in factories. The ends are sold in bales of mixed colors, and the use of them is much deplored by British writers.

How to Figure Wool Requirements

First you must measure the length and width of the area of canvas you wish to cover. If you are figuring background wool, measure the subject's length and width so that you can subtract an approximate amount from the total. Multiply the length by the width in *inches*. Then multiply this total by the number of inches of wool it takes to cover one square inch of canvas.

To figure this amount work a test square inch in your chosen wool and canvas measuring each strand of wool used and then subtracting what is left in the needle. Having multiplied your overall figure by your test patch figure, divide that total by thirty-six to convert back to yards or by sixty to convert back to strands. You will find that each strand of Persian yarn is approximately sixty inches long. If you are using another wool, simply measure a full strand for your division figure. If you are only using two threads of a three-thread strand of Persian, do your arithmetic as if you were using a full strand and then subtract a third of that figure.

Here is an example of how much wool a cushion fourteen by fourteen inches would take. 14 × 14 = 196. Multiply this figure by the number of inches of wool it takes to cover a square inch of a certain canvas, say 50 inches, 50 × 196 = 9800. To reconvert this into yards divide this total by 36, 36 ÷ 9800 = approximately 272 yards. To reconvert into strands divide by 60 (inches) ÷ 9800 = approximately 164 strands of Persian wool.

A standing embroidery frame which belonged to Nelly Custis Lewis. Note the baskets for wool on the main posts. Mrs. Lewis was working on the piece of work in the frame at the time of her death. The frame stands in the upstairs sitting room of her former home, Woodlawn Plantation, Mount Vernon, Virginia. *The National Trust for Historic Preservation.*

FRAMES

XXXXXXXXXXXXXXXXXXXXXXXXXXX
XXXXXXXXXXXXXXXXXXXXXXXXXX

The purpose of using a frame for working needlepoint is to keep the canvas straight and true as biasing stitches are worked on it. Certain stitches, such as the Milanese, the Byzantine and the Scotch, have a strong tendency to distort the canvas, so a frame would be recommended when working them. One has more control over the wool and the needle when using a frame because of the stabbing technique used, with one hand working from the surface and the other hand underneath to receive it. If heirloom quality work is what you want, use a frame, if sheer enjoyment is your aim, don't use one.

Frames work on a scroll principle with two stretchers to keep the scrolls apart. They are called rotating frames if they are not attached to a stand. Canvas no wider than the length of the scroll pieces may be used, so measure your canvas before purchasing one. Frames have a tape tacked to the longest pieces, or have some other means by which canvas can be attached. Pin or stitch the canvas to the tapes and then wind the canvas along the scroll or longest pieces until it is taut. Using carpet thread, lace the sides of the canvas to the shorter side pieces or stretchers, thus creating a trampoline effect. As you complete work, the lacing must be cut, the scrolls turned and refastened and the sides must be relaced. If your frame is a large one, resting it on the arms of a chair may be a comfortable way for you to work, a medium sized frame may be braced against a table and your stomach. If you are making a strip rug and know your stitches tend to bias the canvas, a frame is strongly recommended.

A table frame with ivory trim, a particularly fine piece. *Courtesy The Henry Francis DuPont Winterthur Museum.*

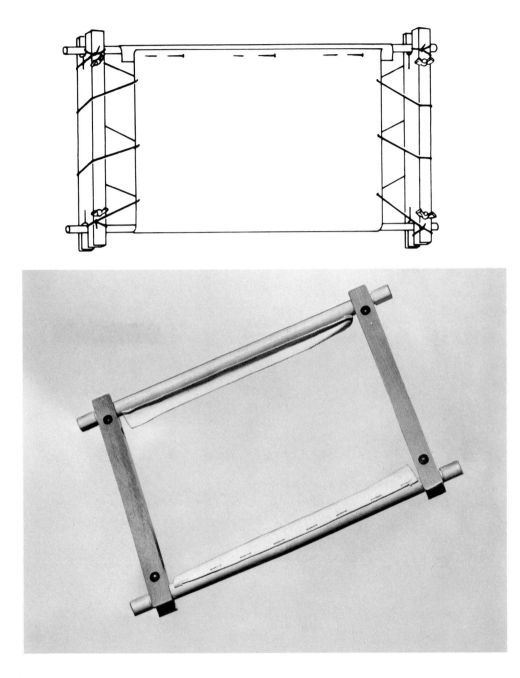

A rotating frame. Note the webbing attached to the long bars.

CAROL PRESTON 1938–1961 HELEN M. SETH-SMITH

The Potomac School banner was designed by Alice Strong and worked by Alice Morgan Carson and Mrs. G. Howland Chase. The names on the bottom of the banner are of the then headmistress and assistant headmistress of the McLean, Virginia, school. Some of the stitches used on the banner which depicts the school buildings, a favorite tree and creek, are the Byzantine, the Jacquard, the Smyrna cross and the Parisian Embroidery stitch.

DESIGN

Sources of Design

Your home is a wonderful source of design ideas. A design from the upholstery of one piece of furniture can be selected and used elsewhere on a cushion or a seatcover. Perhaps there is a repeat design in your drapery material that could be used as a single motif on a foot stool. Part of the pattern of the rug could be copied or even the trim on the fireplace. One small part of a large design could be framed in squares in a checkered design or as a repeat design all by itself. Wall paper designs make fine repeat motifs. Stripes and plaids can be created from the colors used in a room and different fancy stitches can be used to define them. Damask table linen is a good source for dining room chair designs. Pick just one flower design from the dining room rug and repeat it for the chair seats.

Textiles in museums can suggest repeat patterns too. Jacquard designs in particular adapt well to needlepoint because the patterns for Jacquard are designed to be executed stitch by stitch. For designs to be used on cushions, book covers, vests or just as pictures one can use one's hobbies and interests laid out on a plain background. Book illustrations or religious symbols supply design ideas. Doing the family coat of arms is a good idea except that once the relatives see it they will want one. Club emblems and school crests are ideas too. Cross-stitch embroidery books have quite a few adaptable ideas in them. Representations of your home, your pets, favorite flowers and fruits, sports and clubs could be combined or used separately.

Another source of ideas is period furniture, a history of which will not appear here. Period furniture is best seen, not read about, and for design purposes should really not be followed too slavishly. After all, you can buy period canvases already designed, why design what you can buy? Needlepoint went from Cluny-type design (flowers, plants and animals scattered at random on a dark background) to pictorials set in strapping or cartouche, then back to an over-all pattern and finally to large florals. Dark backgrounds predominated in the 16th and 17th century but with the advent of the famous furniture designers of the Georgian period backgrounds became lighter and lighter. The French always seemed to prefer lighter or brighter backgrounds. Bargello was used throughout all of the periods, the original idea coming from the Orient.

If you are doing an original abstract design or a still life arrangement the paper template method of design works very well. Make a paper cutout of each object or shape that will go into the design. Use colored construction paper if possible to get some idea of how the colors will show up on your finished canvas. Move the cutouts around until the design pleases you, glue the pieces into place. Trace the design through a sheet of tracing or layout paper with a felt tip pen or india ink and you are already for the next step, painting it on the canvas.

The point of embroidery is to represent objects in stylized form. One should not be photographically realistic in designing needlepoint. On your first designing attempts, keep it simple, fancy effects and detail will come later. Don't try to put in every shadow and every nuance of color. You don't have to stick to conventional designs in needlepoint, it lends itself very well to today's modern design. Non-realistic nature forms with bold mass color effects are very handsome

The author's first attempt at designing needlepoint: her children and her pets.

done in needlepoint. Just blocks of color or great poppy-like flowers on a solid background can be very effective for pillows or rugs.

Bold design is just right for the use of the fancy stitches, but if the important thing in a design is detail, don't use fancy stitches! Detail in design demands the use of the half cross stitch. Fancy stitches can create special effects in the body or subject of your design. Used in the right proportion to the main design fancy stitches make a fine backgrounding. The kneelers at the Washington Cathedral are a good example of the use of fancy stitches as a backgrounding. The main motif in each one is bold and simple with the upright Gobelin stitch, the slanting Gobelin stitch, the Scotch stitch, and an enlarged Hungarian embroidery stitch used as the backgrounding.

Have some idea of the general outline of your finished product before you begin designing so that everything will fit into the space allowed and there will not be too much space left on the top or bottom. You don't want it to look as if the design had shrunk after it was finished.

Scale is something you must consider in choosing your design for your canvas. A low mesh per inch canvas will not permit much detail of design and shading. Cover your design with various mesh canvases and choose the one that seems to fit or suit the scale of the design the best.

Don't be afraid of color. Use as bright colors as you wish, they will look darker worked up on the canvas. The colors which look bright, even gaudy on the counter, will team up quite tamely on the canvas. If you want a contrast using two shades of the same color, really contrast them. If the contrast is too subtle the colors will look almost the same shade on the canvas.

Keep in mind when laying out your colors what your background color is going to be, this applies to pictorial canvases as well as abstract. You may need a black outline on a figure if there will not be enough contrast with the immediate background color. Sometimes a much lighter shade of the same color as the subject will work, for instance, a light grey outline on a dark grey hippopotamus who is standing on a dark green field. A black outline would be lost in a situation such as this. Some needlepointers prefer to outline with black Filoselle silk when the canvas is finished, making a little back stitch between the other stitches, but this method is apt to look like an afterthought if not carefully handled. When doing landscapes remember that the darker colors are used in the foreground and the lighter shades beyond for distance.

Unless you are designing something that is absolutely flat modern or primitive you will want to have a little depth in your figures. Use three shades of the same color wool to achieve depth in clothing on human figures, the outside edge of the clothing should be darker shades of the rest of the garment. For skin and hair the darker shade would again go on the outside edge, two shades will suffice. Even if you only outline the faces in a darker shade of pink, it will add definition. Animals require only two shades.

For trees you will need three shades of green, the lightest will go on the top of the tree where the sun strikes first, then darker, with the darkest on the bottom where the leaves are presumably in shadow. The first two greens can be used this way on individual branches, with the middle green being used more and more as you come closer to the bottom branches and finally the dark green taking over completely. Three shades of grey or brown are used for the tree trunks, the lightest towards the sun, the darkest towards the shadow. To make a gradual transition of color on the tree trunk, you might try splitting the ply of the two colors you want to combine. Use half a piece of each together as one complete thread.

A seat made by Sarah Tyler in Boston, 1740. *The Metropolitan Museum of Art, Gift of R. Thornton Wilson, 1943, in memory of Florence Ellsworth Wilson.*

The Dot-Dot Effect

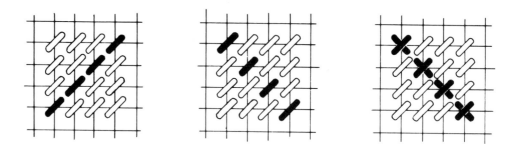

The Dot-Dot Effect Needlepoint has a pecular problem that arises when you design a single diagonal line or outline slanting to the left. It is known as the "dot-dot effect." Because the half cross stitches don't touch head to tail the way they do when slanting a line to the right, gaps appear between the stitches. This creates a broken line of dots or tiny slashes where a complete line is meant to be. There are two ways of correcting this situation, the first is just to design a double line of stitches where you intended to have a single line. The other solution is to go ahead and design your single line, then when you stitch, work the slanting line in cross stitch. Just be sure that the top stroke of the cross stitch is slanting in the same direction as the surrounding half cross stitches. The bottom strokes of the cross stitches will connect head to tail, thereby creating a straight unbroken line for you.

For great detail one can use petit point on the same canvas as gros point but only on penelope canvas (as opposed to one thread or mono-canvas). To do petit point on penelope canvas just separate the two warp threads and the two woof threads and use it as one would mono-canvas. The petit point will thus be one quarter the size of the gros point stitches. You will see this done on antique needle-point in museums, especially for faces in pictorial canvases. One can add petit point to mono-canvas by insetting or appliquéing a piece of petit point canvas or gauze.

When it comes to framing needlepoint pictures one rarely uses a mat, especially a paper one. To make a picture canvas look more "finished," one can make a border of fancy stitches, or a border of half cross stitch in another color. The wood frame would go around this. When doing a needlepoint coat of arms ask your framer to put a gold liner on the inside edge of the frame. A gold border painted on the glass is elegant but it is also very expensive.

If you are designing a chair seat, measure how high the padding rises from the frame and add that much to all the sides of your canvas. You want the finished product to fit.

There are two methods of appliquéing, first the obvious one of sewing in the appliqué, and the other of tying it in. The sewing method is recommended for the finer meshes and for pieces of canvas which are of a widely different size mesh. Tying in is very hard on the eyes and should not be attempted for anything under fourteen mesh to the inch. Designing for appliqué is quite difficult. Keep detail on the outside outline of the appliqué to an absolute minimum, make curves gradual. Corners are not to be feared as they can be mitred. The instructions for appliquéing are to be found in a later chapter.

A bell pull showing an interesting use of the bargello stitch, probably made in the 18th century. *Courtesy, Mrs. George Maurice Morris.*

An antique child's chair with oyster pattern covering. *Courtesy, Mrs. Roman V. Mrozinski.*

Methods of Transferring the Design to Canvas

There are two schools of thought on the best way to transfer design to canvas: graph paper charts versus painting on canvas. For the novice designer the graph paper method of laying out a design is the most foolproof way as well as the most educational way. You can see just what the design will look like blocked out stitch by stitch. Curves are easier to handle and errors easier to correct. You are less apt to go in for hair by hair realism on graph paper because it does have to be blocked out stitch by stitch.

Needlepoint looks best when used for mass rather than detail. As you grow more proficient at designing you will add more detail, particularly if you try your hand at a petit point piece where there is more room for detail. Some people find it is easier on their eyes to look at the graph paper design rather than two shades of the same color, that is, the painted canvas with the same shade wool on top.

On the other hand, a canvas with the design painted on it is much more portable for working on wherever you like. The graph paper method needs to be done at home where you can concentrate on counting off your design. Perhaps it boils down to whether you want to think about the needlepoint as you do it or not. If you have had some experience with painting by all means use the painted canvas method; otherwise, try the graph paper way first.

Graph Paper The school variety of graph paper is the simplest to use because it has the squares already counted off into fives or tens. Each square counts as one stitch. If the size of your finished product is limited draw its outline in light-colored crayon on the canvas, or baste its outline in cotton sewing thread. Count the number of meshes from right to left inside the outline, and the number from top to bottom. Count off the same number of squares, right to left, top to bottom, on the graph paper and draw your outline on it. It does not matter if the scale is different, it's the mesh number that counts.

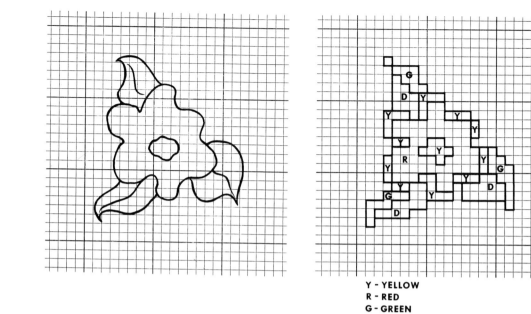

Y - YELLOW
R - RED
G - GREEN
D - DARK GREEN

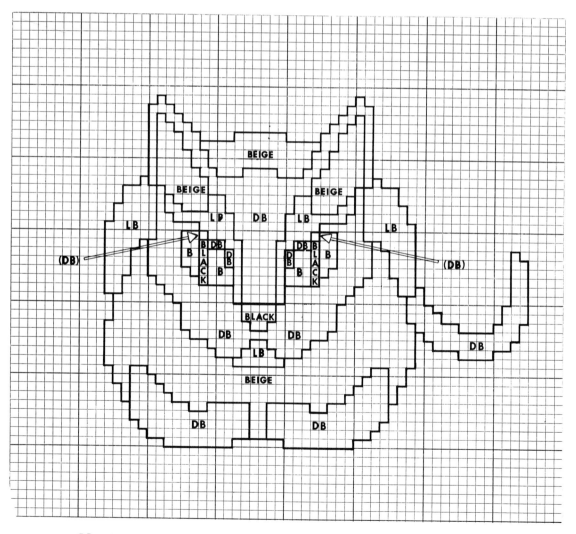

DB - DARK BROWN

LB - LIGHT BROWN

B - BLUE

Sketch your design right on the graph paper as though it had no cross hatching on it. Then, following the lines of your sketch, block in the stitches, by the square, keeping as close to the sketch line as possible. Color the pattern with colored pencils or colored inks. To start work on the canvas you must count off the mesh to find the exact center horizontally, mark it with crayon or basting thread. Then count off to find the center vertically and mark it. Mark your graph design the same way, remembering that EACH SQUARE REPRE-SENTS ONE STITCH. You will find that these center markings will aid you in your countings as you work on your designs. Start work right in the center of the canvas working out to the edges.

Painting on the Canvas   There are several different ways of actually applying your design to the canvas and they all involve making a cartoon. "Cartoon" is a tapestry term which means making a drawing of your design in scale usually without color. If you need to enlarge your design now is the time to do it. A photographer can enlarge it for you to the exact size you need. Give him a tracing of it done in felt tip pen or if it is very small in ball point pen. This is the most expen-sive way of enlarging the design but also the most accurate.

The cheaper way of enlarging is to cover a pencilled tracing of the design with vertical and horizontal lines an even distance away from each other. On a larger piece of paper measure out the outline of the size you wish the finished product to be. Draw the same number of vertical and horizontal lines on the larger paper as you had on the first. Now draw the contents of each of the smaller squares into the exact same one of the larger paper. (See diagram)

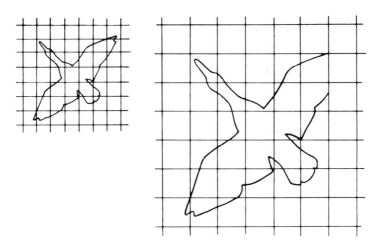

Now that your cartoon is ready it is time to choose which medium to use. The simplest way is wax crayons. This medium works best with very simple undetailed designs. Because it is a dry medium it is an excellent technique for children.

Tack your cartoon to a drawing board. To make the design easier to see through the canvas, outline the cartoon with a felt tip pen. Tack the canvas over the cartoon, lining the canvas threads up with the straight lines of your cartoon outline. Be sure you leave a margin of bare canvas of one and a half to two inches around all edges of the canvas, you will need it later in the finishing process. Then trace the design with the crayons either outlining it or coloring it all in, whichever you prefer. Remove the canvas from the drawing board and place it on a paper towel. Place another paper towel over it and with an iron set on cotton, gently iron it. Don't iron too long or you will take all the wax off, you only want to remove the excess. You may stitch on it immediately.

A design idea taken with few changes from a greeting card. The cross stitch, leaf stitch, Byzantine stitch, and interlocking Gobelin stitch were used on the rooster. LEFT: *card reproduced by permission of Hallmark*; RIGHT: *courtesy Victor R. Forte, Jr., worked by the author.*

Paint is the most professional method of applying the design to canvas, it will allow for the most detail. Most shops use acrylic paints because they are mixed with water and dry very quickly. Oil paints are the time honored method, they are much slower to dry but do permit a greater degree of shading. If all other factors are equal choose the medium with which you are most used to working.

Acrylic paints should be mixed to the consistency of coffee cream. If it is too thin the paint will run along the canvas thread like a wick, if too thick, the mesh of the canvas becomes clogged. The paint will dry solid and in pricking out the clogged mesh, the paint is apt to pop off the canvas entirely. Thin oil paint with a tiny bit of turpentine and a few drops of Japan dryer or Grumbacher's Textine by itself. The dryer and Textine will make the paints dry a little faster, the dryer will cause the colors to darken a bit. The consistency of the oils should be a little thicker than coffee cream, not so thick as to clog the mesh. It may take as long as forty-eight hours for oils to dry; if you are impatient to get the stitching part, perhaps acrylics should be your paint medium.

The cartoon should be tacked to the drawing board as one does for crayoning, and the canvas tacked over it lining up the canvas threads with the straight lines of the design. Use fine brushes, except when you are filling in large areas of color, then larger ones may be used if you wish. The BIG SECRET of needlepoint canvas painting is to apply just one color of paint per intersection of canvas. Sketching just won't do for needlepoint, you must be precise. The point is to make the canvas easy to stitch, and if you have to stop at each mesh to try to figure out which color is meant the fun is soon gone. The signs of a well-painted canvas are clearly defined colors on each mesh, and little paint showing through on the back of the canvas, thus proving that the consistency of the paint was just right.

Marking pens are a risky medium to use for needlepoint because so many brands are not waterproof. Some claim to be but really are not. The significance of their fastness is that in blocking the finished canvas, some water is used. If the paint medium is not waterproof it will run into the wool, creating a mess. To test a marker (or any medium) dab some color on the canvas. Let it dry for about half an hour and then lay a wet paper towel over it. Allow half an hour to pass and then check it. If it ran, do not use it. It is a good idea to check the wool you use too, put a snip of it on a paper towel and drip water on it. Check it again in half an hour to see if it ran.

Incidentally, Scotch-Gard, cleaning fluid or martinis will make practically any medium run if the canvas is flooded with it. To protect against such accidents, a coat of clear plastic spray over the painted canvas will help or paint it with polymer gloss medium. The latter will give a very professional gloss to the finished canvas.

Transfers   If the idea of tracing the design on the canvas does not appeal to you, an iron-on transfer may be the answer. Outline your design with a felt-tipped pen on a piece of layout paper and then turn it over. With the design face down, trace your design again as it gleams through the layout paper, using your transfer medium this time. The reason for all this tracing and retracing is to avoid reversing the direction of your design, important if there is any writing in the design. Transfer mediums available are crewel transfer pencils (get an aqua-colored one, not the fuchsia) and embroidery paints such as Artex and Deco Write. Use a light color of embroidery paint because dark paint will "shine" through wool worked over it, spoiling the effect of the stitches.

Tack your canvas on to a drawing board and place the design over it, transfer side down. Using a cotton setting on your iron, slowly move the iron over the paper, lingering perhaps ten or fifteen seconds over each area. Before you remove the transfer, peek to make sure the transfer is taking. The disadvantages of this technique are the aforementioned shining through of the outline color, the difficulty in achieving any degree of fine detail and the fact that straight lines are difficult to match up with the threads of the canvas, thus limiting the technique to more or less curvy designs. Having transferred the design to canvas you can now either paint in the colors or stitch them in. Commercially made transfers should be applied to the canvas according to their directions, but ironing on a drawing board is still a good idea.

The silk screen process is another way of applying design to canvas but it is practical only in terms of quantity production and is therefore beyond the scope of this book.

A painted canvas. The design is from an oriental rug and was the first painting effort of Helene Bress, noted weaver and author.

Mrs. Charles Hight of Rome, Georgia, designed and worked the needle-point bird picture. She used the brick stitch and the kalem stitch to add texture to the bird's feathers. The bird is in shades of green and brown.

THE STITCHES

The most efficient way to learn the stitches is to do them. Then you can see just how they will look for your design purposes. Seeing a picture or diagram in a book just does not tell the relative size to other stitches or the contrasting textures. Working a sampler is really an excellent way to make these discoveries. It is also a permanent record of the stitches that you are not liable to give away as you would with finished items. All you need to make a sampler is half a yard or less of mono-canvas, less than that of a two thread canvas, needles and about four ounces of yarn. Bind the edges of the canvas with binding tape or masking tape and you are all set to go. A dressmakers' chalk will mark off squares if you want to make a precise sampler, or you can just mix them random style. You will find as you work that design ideas will suggest themselves to you, so write them down; you'll surely forget them otherwise. A sampler will show you just which stitches are the wool eaters, and which bias the canvas. Keep in mind when you choose your sampler wool colors that light colors show texture best.

There are two ways of threading a needle with wool. One is to fold the wool and, pinching it between the thumb and forefinger, push the bend of the fold through the eye of the needle. With your fingernails pull it through the eye of the needle, making sure all of the fibers come through. The other way is to trim the end of the wool with the scissors, and this time squeezing it with the thumb and forefinger nails, force it through the eye. This is a good way to thread the needle if you have too much wool to fit the eye of the needle.

A trick well worth cultivating as you work your stitches, is to twirl the needle between your thumb and fingers about every ten stitches or so. This occasional twirling will help keep the wool threads aligned and not twisted too tightly around each other. This will insure more even looking stitches.

Wool wears thin from being pulled through the canvas too many times, and this results in uneven looking stitches. It is advisable therefore to use reasonably short lengths of wool in the needle. Use a foot of wool in your needle for petit point, about eighteen inches for the middle range of mesh, and just a few inches more for rug wool on rug canvas. To make this more convenient, why not cut your wool into those lengths when you buy it. Tie the colors into separate bundles to keep them from becoming tangled, or snap them into upholsterer's snap tape if you have many colors.

To start any stitch you insert the needle into the face of the canvas about an inch from where you really mean to start but in the path of your intended stitches. Then bring the needle up at the real starting point. Pull the wool almost through the canvas, leaving just a little tag sticking up on the front of the canvas. As you stitch, make an effort to work over that piece of wool on the back of the canvas so that it will be firmly lashed down. Pull the little tag left in front through to the back when you feel the back piece has been secured sufficiently. Never start by knotting the wool!

If your piece of canvas is large and you find it cumbersome to hold, roll up the sides as you would a scroll. Pin the rolls near the top and bottom, being careful not to split a canvas thread with the pin. Leave three or four inches unrolled in the center where you are going to work. Unpin and reroll as you work.

Keep the tension on your wool as even as you can. Uneven tension in needlepoint shows up just as much as it does in knitting. Stitches that are too tight will allow bare canvas to show through, stitches that are consistently too tight will pull the canvas way out of

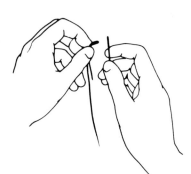

Threading Needle

"Mary of Scotland Mourning over the Dying Douglas" from a painting by Landseer. It measures four feet by five and one half feet. The picture is one of the better examples of Berlin woolwork and was done sometime in the latter part of the 19th century. Paper patterns and bright wools from Berlin were much in vogue for needlework during the Victorian era, hence the name Berlin woolwork. *The Smithsonian Institution, Washington, D.C.*

shape, beyond repair by stretching. When your canvas is finished and you find an occasional loose stitch here and there, just pull on the back of the stitch with your needle to draw up the slack.

To finish off a thread, run the needle through the just completed stitches on the back of the canvas, about an inch will do. The reason for finishing off a thread on its own completed stitches is to minimize trouble if ever you should need to snip out a mistake. Cut the completed thread close to the canvas. Keep the back of your canvas as neat as possible, otherwise you will be stitching in bits of color from the back to the front from nearby tag ends. The thread you are working with is apt to get snarled with tag ends from the back if they are not clipped close.

An eighteenth century wing chair; the covering is unusual in that, though the pattern is a typical bargello one, the stitch is the kalem stitch. *Courtesy, Mrs. George Maurice Morris.*

Two of the following stitches have tramé as a base. It might be well to explain now just what it is. Some canvases are sold with the background and possibly the subject done in a long horizontal basting-like stitch. This is tramé. It is used on these canvases to show what colors to use and to indicate the design. The right amount of wool and the right colors of wool are included with this type of canvas as a sort of kit. One stitches right over the tramé as though it were not even there. It is an understitching. It must be laid on in irregular series, as it will form ridges if done in regular rows. Tramé may also be used to add body to a stitch, to beef it up, and this is its purpose with the stitches included here. To figure the extra wool needed to tramé, just halve the number of mesh per inch of the canvas you are using and add two inches to the figure for each square inch. Thus if you are using fourteen mesh canvas, half of fourteen is seven plus the two added inches equals nine extra inches of wool for each square inch of tramé.

The following table lists suggested uses for the stitches. It is just a guide line for you to follow until you are familiar enough with the stitches to make your own judgments on them. The word filling means a stitch to be used in an enclosed area, not the background.

Only stitches which adequately cover the canvas have been included in the following collection. In tapestry no warp threads are allowed to show through, so why let canvas show through in needlepoint? No stitch combinations have been included, just the fundamental stitch. Think up your own combinations, as there are literally hundreds of them.

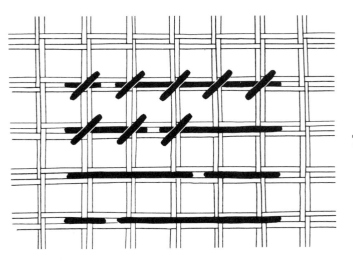

Tramé on penelope canvas

	filling	back-ground	grounding, striking pattern by itself	detail, single specimen	slow to work up	quick to work up	best on mono-canvas	best on two-thread canvas
The Rep Stitch	×				×			×
The Cross Stitch	×	×			×			×
The Cross Stitch Tramé	×				×			×
The Oblong Cross Stitch	×					×		×
The Oblong Cross Stitch with Back Stitch	×				×			×
The Upright Cross Stitch	×	×				×	×	
The Smyrna Cross Stitch	×		×	×	×		×	×
The Double Cross Stitch	×					×	×	
The Double Stitch	×	×	×			×		×
The Rice Stitch	×			×	×			×
The Double Straight Cross Stitch	×		×			×	×	
The Double Leviathan Stitch	×		×		×		×	×
The Greek Stitch	×			×		×	×	×
The Long Armed Cross Stitch	×			×		×	×	×
The Diagonal Long Armed Cross Stitch	×				×		×	×
The Closed Cat Stitch			×			×	×	×
The Running Cross Stitch				×		×		×
The Tied Down Cross Stitch	×		×	×		×	×	×
The Woven Cross Stitch Square			×	×	×		×	×
The Woven Cross Stitch			×		×		×	×
The Fancy Cross Stitch			×	×		×	×	×
The Triple Cross Stitch				×		×	×	

	filling	back-ground	grounding, striking pattern by itself	detail, single specimen	slow to work up	quick to work up	best on mono-canvas	best on two-thread canvas
The Check Stitch			×			×	×	
The French Diagonal Stitch	×		×			×	×	
The Herringbone Stitch	×		×		×			×
The Reverse Herringbone Stitch	×		×		×			×
The Two-Color Herringbone Stitch			×			×		×
The Plaited Gobelin Stitch			×			×		×
The Bazar Stitch			×		×			×
The Velvet Stitch	×				×			×
The Fern Stitch	×					×	×	×
The Long and Short Oblique Stitch			×			×		×
The Point de Tresse Stitch			×	×	×		×	×
The French Stitch	×		×		×			×
The Knotted Stitch	×				×		×	×
The Rococo Stitch	×		×	×	×		×	×
The Diagonal Shell Stitch			×		×		×	
The Roumanian Stitch	×					×	×	
The Gobelin Stitch	×	×				×	×	
The Renaissance Stitch	×				×			×
The Gobelin Tramé Stitch	×		×			×		×
The Brick Stitch	×	×				×	×	
The Irish Stitch		×	×			×	×	
Bargello		×	×			×	×	

	filling	back-ground	grounding, striking pattern by itself	detail, single specimen	slow to work up	quick to work up	best on mono-canvas	best on two-thread canvas
The Old Florentine Stitch			×			×	×	
The Parisian Embroidery Stitch	×	×	×			×	×	
The Hungarian Embroidery Stitch	×	×	×			×	×	
The Enlarged Parisian Embroidery Stitch			×			×	×	
The Slanting Gobelin Stitch	×	×				×	×	×
The Wicker Stitch	×		×			×	×	
The Interlocking Gobelin Stitch	×				×		×	×
The Encroaching Oblique Stitch	×	×				×	×	×
The Oblique Slav Stitch	×					×	×	×
The Kalem Stitch or the Knit Stitch	×	×				×	×	×
The Diagonal Knit Stitch	×	×				×	×	×
The Mosaic Stitch	×	×	×			×	×	×
The Mosaic Stitch Done Diagonally	×	×	×			×	×	×
The Scotch Stitch	×		×			×	×	×
The Checker Stitch		×	×			×	×	×
The Point Russe Stitch				×		×	×	×
The Scotch Stitch Worked Diagonally		×	×			×	×	×
The Moorish Stitch		×	×			×	×	×
The Cashmere Stitch	×	×	×			×	×	×
The Cashmere Stitch Worked Diagonally	×	×	×			×	×	×

	filling	back-ground	grounding, striking pattern by itself	detail, single specimen	slow to work up	quick to work up	best on mono-canvas	best on two-thread canvas
The Milanese Stitch		×	×			×	×	×
The Oriental Stitch		×	×			×	×	×
The Byzantine Stitch		×	×			×	×	×
The Jacquard Stitch		×	×			×	×	×
The Web Stitch	×				×		×	
The Stem Stitch	×		×		×		×	×
The Perspective Stitch			×	×	×		×	×
The Leaf Stitch	×	×	×	×		×	×	×
The Star Stitch	×				×		×	
The Eye Stitch	×		×	×	×		×	×
The Ray Stitch	×				×		×	×
The Diamond Eyelet Stitch	×		×		×		×	×
The Reverse Eyelet Stitch	×			×		×	×	×
The Triangle Stitch			×	×		×	×	
The Triple Leviathan Stitch			×	×	×		×	
The Flower Stitch				×		×	×	
The Surrey Stitch	×		×			×	×	×
Turkey Work	×		×			×	×	×
The Raised Work Stitch	×		×			×	×	×
The Chain Stitch	×				×		×	
The Laced Chain Stitch	×		×			×	×	×
The Darning Stitch	×		×		×		×	

The Half Cross Stitch

The basic stitch in needlepoint or canvas work is a short slanting stitch worked over one intersection of the canvas mesh. It is called the half cross stitch because it is half of a cross stitch, a cross stitch is two slanting stitches worked in the opposite directions to each other over one intersection of the canvas mesh. There are three ways of working the half cross stitch. They all achieve the same effect on the face of the canvas; it is only on the back of the canvas that you can determine the method used. All of the half cross stitches have aliases (this goes for the fancy stitches too). To clarify this situation the most popular name is given first with the other names following.

From the number of initials on the motif sampler it would appear that a group of friends all took part in making it. Many colors were used in the figures, the background is black, and the stitch is the half cross. *The Smithsonian Institution, Washington, D.C.*

The Continental Stitch or Tent Stitch

The continental stitch is shown first because one uses it in working the basket weave stitch. This stitch is best used for working small details and single vertical or horizontal lines of stitches. The reason it is not used for large areas is that it biases the canvas quite badly. You will find that stitches that slant both on the face and the back of the canvas usually are biasers, the canvas is more or less tied into a slanted position. Working the continental stitch in a frame will correct the bias.

The continental stitch is worked from right to left, then the canvas is turned upside down to work the next row. With the continental stitch, the needle slants diagonally under two canvas threads, as you complete one stitch you are setting yourself up for the next stitch. It works well on all of the canvases.

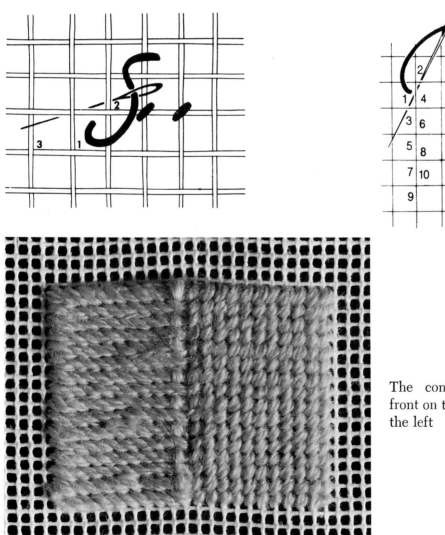

The continental stitch, the front on the right, the back on the left

The Basket Weave Stitch or Bias Tent Stitch or the Diagonal Stitch

The basket weave stitch is the preferred half cross stitch. It should be used whenever possible, for subject matter as well as backgrounds. Its great virtue is that it does not bias the canvas. It is also easier to work in that one does not have to keep turning the canvas around and around. The importance of preventing bias is to minimize the amount of blocking the canvas will need at completion. A badly biased canvas may take more than one blocking to straighten it out and may never block completely straight. Try to use the basket weave as much as possible, keeping the use of the continental to a minimum. The basket weave has a firm backing which looks as if it had been woven, hence its name. It can be worked on all canvases.

The needle passes under two canvas threads for such stitch, horizontally on an up row, and vertically on a down row. A continental-like stitch at the end of each row will help you finish your present row and start you off on the next row (see diagram A & B).

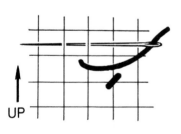

Needle always goes under two mesh horizontally on 'up' row.

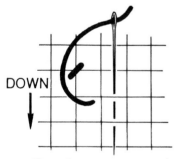

Needle always goes under two mesh vertically on 'down' row.

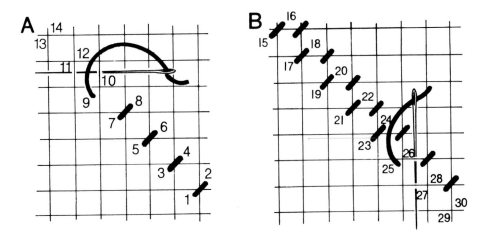

There is a unique way to finish off your thread with the basket weave stitch that will prevent those unsightly ridges that one sees when the light falls on the canvas wrong. On your last stitch simply take your needle through to the back of the canvas and then bring it out about an inch from where you went in. Leave a little tag of wool hanging on the face of the canvas. As you work subsequent rows, you will slowly cover up the wool left on the back of the canvas, pull the tag on the face through to the back when you reach it. Looking at the back of your work it will be very difficult to see where a thread started or finished.

If you must leave your work at the end of a row and you can't remember whether you are on a down or up row, look on the back of the canvas to see if the last row left vertical or horizontal stitches on the back. If horizontal, then you know your next row is a down row, if vertical, the next row is an up row. This is important, because if you work two consecutive rows in the same direction an odd high line of stitches is the result.

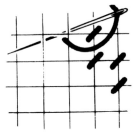

Continental stitch at end of 'up' row ends that row and begins the next.

Vertical continental stitch finishes 'down' row and starts the next row.

The basket weave stitch, the front on the right, the back on the left

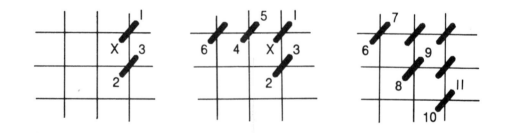

How to start the basket weave stitch in a corner

Quick Point or The Half Cross Stitch

Quick point is the simplest of the half cross stitches. It is nothing more than a whip stitch done on canvas. It biases the canvas quite badly, which is its chief fault; a lesser fault is that it cannot be worked on mono-canvas. Try it and you will see, the wool slides about without the two-thread weave to hold it firmly in place.

It is worked from left to right; when one row is done, turn the canvas upside down and start the next row. It is simple enough for small children to learn and has the added advantage for them of allowing them to work from bottom to top if they prefer. When they are older they can be taught the basket weave.

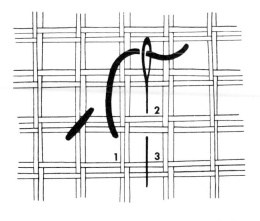

Quick point, the front on the right, the back on the left

The Rep Stitch or the Aubusson Stitch

This stitch is really a variation of the quick point stitch. It can be worked only on a two thread or penelope canvas, then it is stitched over both warp threads and only one of the weft. The result has the look of rep silk. It does bias the canvas.

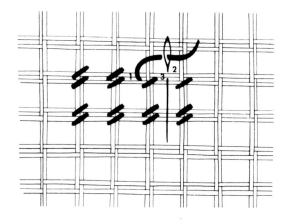

The Cross Stitch

The cross stitch was much used by our ancestors for their pictorial needlepoint pictures, it was also a favorite of early English needlepointers. The cross stitch can be worked on all canvases, though it looks best on the two-thread variety. You will need less wool in your needle than you would if you were working the half cross stitch. For instance, if you use a full strand of Persian for the half cross stitch, for the cross stitch two threads will probably suffice. Some people prefer to work a row of half cross stitch and then return, crossing the half crosses as you come, so to speak. The single trip method here diagramed is recommended for mono-canvas. The important thing to remember with the cross stitch is to make sure all the crosses cross in the same direction. There are several variations of this stitch, but this is the basic one.

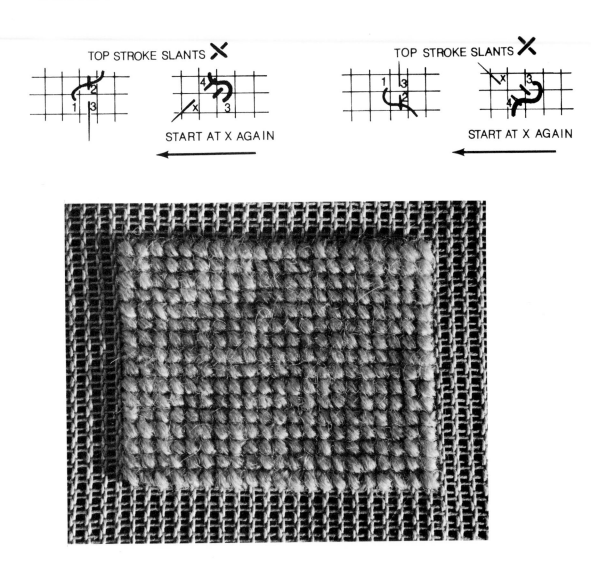

The Cross Stitch Tramé

The cross stitch from a distance looks very much like plain old half cross stitch, but a cross stitch tramé cannot be mistaken this way. It sits up on its understitching and the cross is quite obvious. It is appropriate to use when a fine texture is not required. When doing the tramé understitching do be sure that you are *not* doing it evenly. Make some of your long stitches over five warp threads, then over six and seven. It is important not to have a pattern of tramé stitches showing through the cross stitches. This cross stitch is the same as the one before except that it is done over two mesh each way. Don't forget to make all the crosses in the same direction.

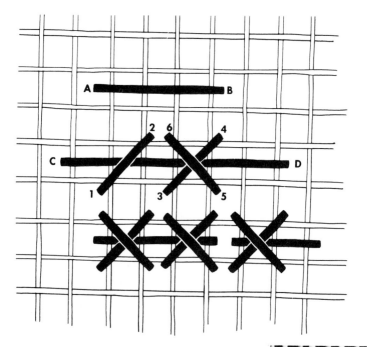

The Oblong Cross Stitch

The oblong cross stitch is a tall cross stitch which can be done on both canvases. On mono-canvas it looks a little like rope, on penelope the crosses are more obvious. It is a hard stitch to keep uniform, the crosses tend to straggle unless the tension is even on each stitch. This stitch does not provide much of a backing. Don't forget to make all the crosses in the same direction.

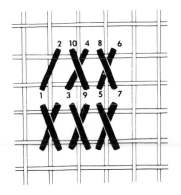

The Oblong Cross Stitch with Back Stitch

This stitch is almost the same as the previous stitch. You might call this one a tall cross stitch with a belt. If you require a very hard wearing, rough feeling stitch, here it is. It is sort of knotty looking, and is not at all apt to snag. This stitch is similar in appearance to the knotted stitch but they are constructed differently. This stitch is slow to work up, does not pull the canvas out of shape, and does have a very firm backing. Its major fault is that it is a wool-eater.

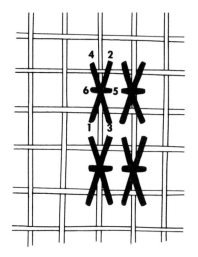

The Upright Cross Stitch

The upright cross stitch gives a pin seal leather-like look. It is a tough stitch and hard to snag. It is useful for subject as well as backgrounding. It does not bias the canvas. If the first two or three rows of this stitch don't look like much of anything, persist, and by about the sixth or seventh row it will start taking shape. Use a little less wool in your needle than you would ordinarily. If you stitch it diagonally as shown here, you will find that it works up rather quickly.

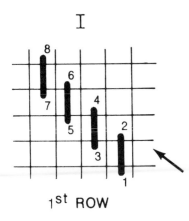

I

1st ROW

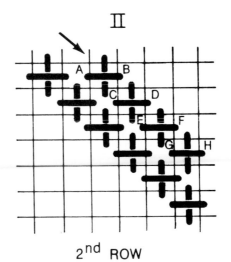

II

2nd ROW

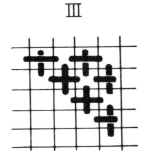

III

Fitting the stitch
in a corner

The Smyrna Cross Stitch

The Smyrna cross stitch is one of needlepoint's most versatile stitches. It is not only decorative and highly textured, but it is functional too. It can be used to join two pieces of canvas. Just place one edge of canvas over the other, matching mesh for mesh, baste them together, and then work the Smyrna cross stitch over the whole business. The bulk of the stitch neatly covers the cut edges of the top layer of canvas. Its only drawback is that you cannot work half a Smyrna cross stitch; the area in which it is used must be divisible by two both ways. Be sure all the top stitches are worked in the same direction.

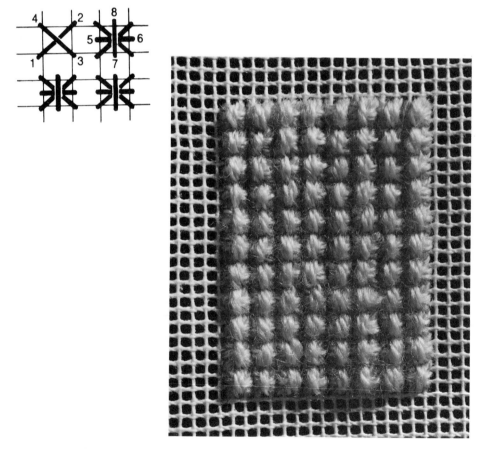

The Double Cross Stitch

The double cross stitch really could be called the two cross stitch. This would be a better description since this stitch is really a combination of the cross stitch and the upright cross stitch. The wool must fit the canvas exactly for this stitch, just fat enough, otherwise canvas will show through. The double cross stitch is attractive done in one color; it is also attractive with the cross stitch done in one color and the upright cross done in another color. Don't forget to watch the direction of your crosses.

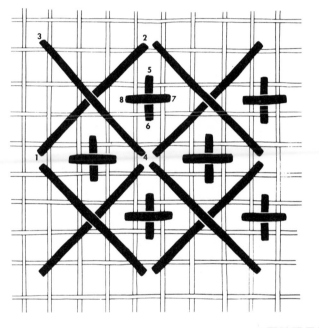

The Double Stitch

The double stitch is very like the double cross stitch in name and the way it is done. The big difference is that the big cross stitch is a long cross stitch. This is a difficult stitch to work on fine canvas. It is recommended that you use it on ten mesh or lower. Work the large crosses first and then fill in with the little ones. The result is a neat woven effect that is heightened if you work the little crosses in another color. Watch your cross direction.

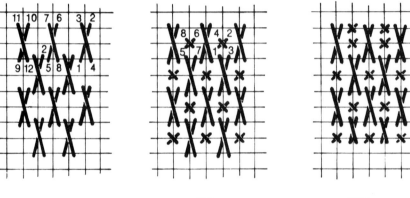

I   II   III

The Rice Stitch or the Crossed Corners Stitch or the William and Mary Stitch

The rice stitch is another one that must have the wool fitting exactly if the stitch is to be effective at all. You must experiment until you are satisfied that no canvas shows through the wool but that at the same time the stitch does not look too crowded. The rice stitch is really just the cross stitch with its arms tied down. Try doing the cross stitch in one color and the tie-downs in another shade of the same color.

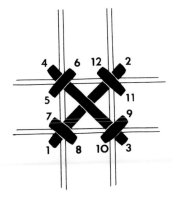

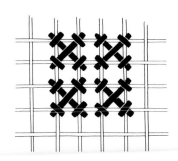

The Double Straight Cross Stitch

This stitch is very similar to the upright cross stitch. The big difference is that the double straight cross stitch must be worked over four mesh each way and it has an extra cross to hold it down. It is very important to fit the wool to the canvas just so or the canvas will show through. Make sure all of your little crosses are going in the same direction.

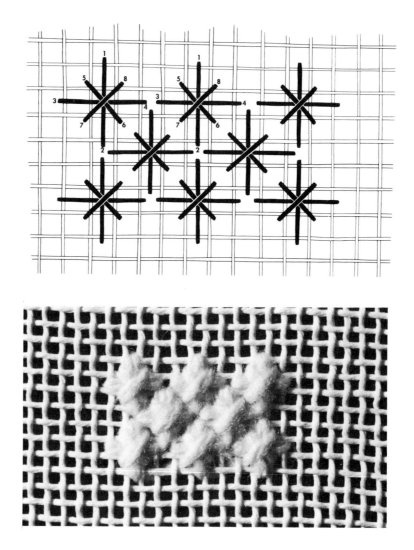

The Double Leviathan Stitch

The double leviathan stitch may be used in rows or as a separate decorative stitch. A single square of the stitch makes quite a high bump on the canvas, very much like the popcorn stitch in crochet. If necessary to cover the canvas a long upright stitch may be used between the squares of stitches. When designing the space for this stitch make sure it is divisible by four since this stitch does not halve very well.

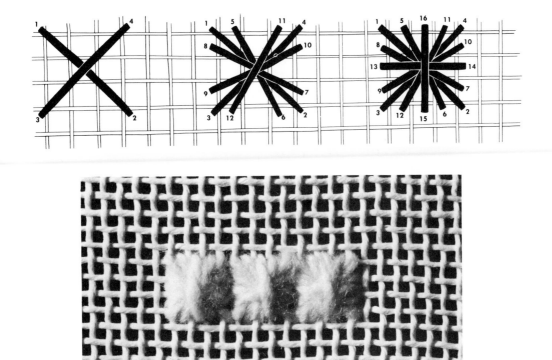

The Greek Stitch and
the Long Armed Cross Stitch

These stitches look alike from the front of the canvas, it is only from
the back of the canvas that one can tell which stitch was used. The
long armed cross stitch is a little clumsy to work, though the Portu-
guese seem to prefer it. They make a special kind of rug on a jute
canvas using the stitch exclusively, which are called Arriaolos rugs.
Both stitches form a thin braid, very nice for borders. If you work
multiple stripes of it, they should all point in the same direction.

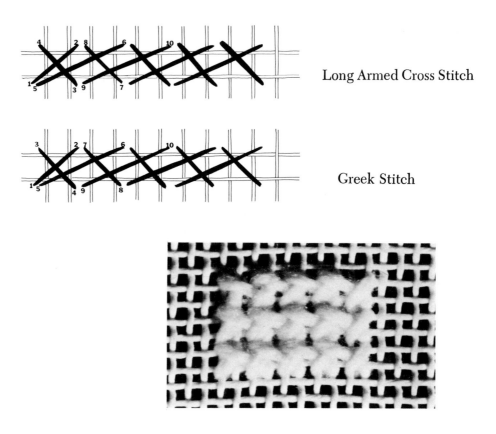

Long Armed Cross Stitch

Greek Stitch

The Diagonal Long Armed Cross Stitch

This stitch makes a nice companion to the Greek version of the previous stitch. It is a little tricky to catch on to at first, but once you have
the rhythm of it you are all set. It makes a firm braid on the face of the
canvas and like the previous stitch has little wool on the back. It does
bias the canvas. A frame would be advisable for large areas of the
stitch.

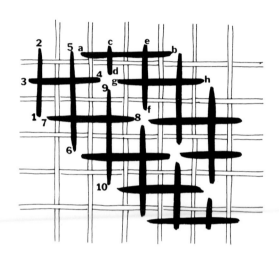

The Closed Cat Stitch or the Telescoped Herringbone Stitch

This stitch is really just a variation of the long armed cross stitch or the herringbone stitch; compare the diagrams. It makes a tight, hard ridge-like braid, as a grounding it looks like corduroy. It may be worked over two or three mesh and it does not bias the canvas.

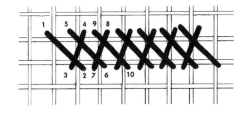

The Running Cross Stitch or the Long Cross Stitch

The running cross stitch works best on a two-thread canvas, but it is unusual in that it can be worked over just one set of mesh instead of two. It serves very well between rows of Gobelin stitch or Roumanian stitch, stitches that otherwise show canvas on their outer edges. It makes a high ridged braid and is so easy to work. If used as a single braid use the normal amount of wool, if used in multiple rows use about half the amount you usually would.

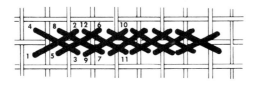

The Tied Down Cross Stitch

This stitch is a Victorian stitch that was used by itself to embellish a field of half cross stitches. It can be used as grounding, however, as shown here. You will need less wool in your needle when used as a grounding, alternating colors give it more definition. It is worked in diagonal rows. Be sure that all the top crosses cross in the same direction.

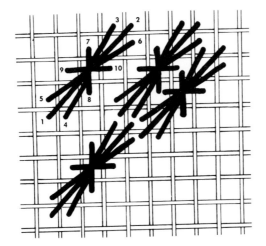

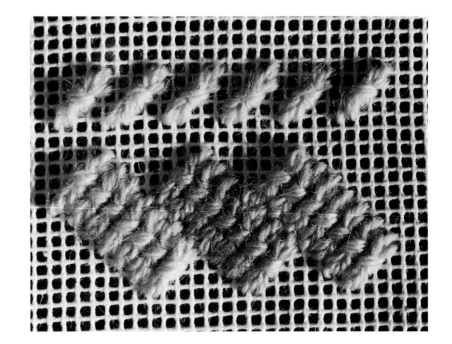

The Woven Cross Stitch Square and the Woven Cross Stitch

The woven cross stitch square version of this stitch may be worked as a specimen that is all by itself in a field of half cross stitches or as a grounding. When used as a grounding it is very attractive worked in two colors. Be sure you weave all the crosses alike. You will probably need more wool in your needle than usual to cover the canvas.

    The woven cross stitch itself can also be used as a grounding but the spaces on the sides must be filled in with half cross stitches. This stitch also will need more wool to cover the canvas.

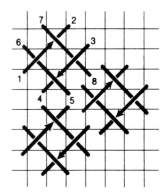

The Woven Cross Stitch as a grounding.

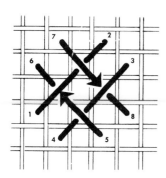

The Woven Cross Stitch Square

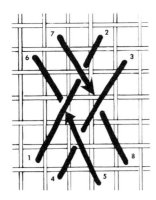

The Woven Cross Stitch

The Fancy Cross Stitch

This stitch is reminiscent of the double straight cross stitch and the Smyrna cross stitch. It dates from the late 19th century when stitches were apt to be big and sprawly. This one is; it makes a very busy grounding. The wool must fit the canvas just right or the canvas will show through around the largest cross stitches. Experiment until you have enough wool in your needle. Make the smaller cross stitches in another color. Make sure all your cross stitches cross in the same direction.

The Triple Cross Stitch

This cross stitch is just a specimen stitch and a very pretty one, too. The background of half cross stitch must be worked first because the cross stitch itself reaches out into the background. The very long strokes are worked right into the first row of half cross stitch. (See diagram.) Leave a bare spot of canvas six mesh high by two mesh wide in the form of a Greek or "red" cross. Make the cross stitch a different color than the background for the best results.

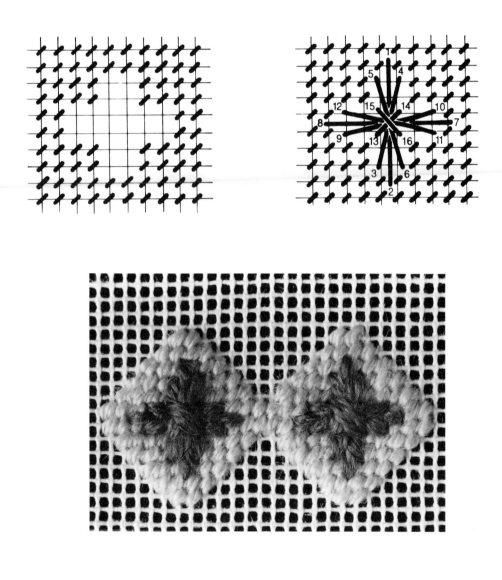

The Check Stitch

The check stitch is another super big cross stitch which looks very tweedy when worked as a grounding. If worked in diagonal rows alternating colors each stitch one can achieve a checked effect. Surprisingly you will not need more wool in your needle. Since the stitch does not halve well the space for it should be carefully planned. Be sure that you cross the stitch the same way each time.

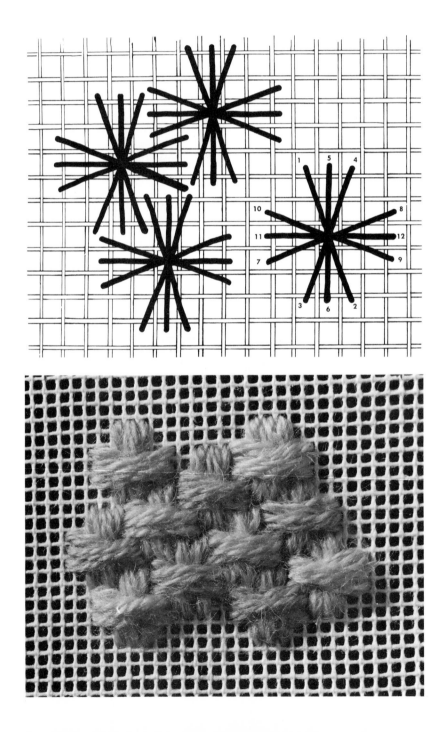

The Diagonal French Stitch

This stitch is a tall cousin of the upright cross; the result is quite different. The French diagonal stitch looks as if it were couched, as one does in crewel. It does not take any more wool than usual on mono-canvas and leno canvas but you have to add more if you use it on two thread canvas. Work the long stitches first and then go back up the row and cross them.

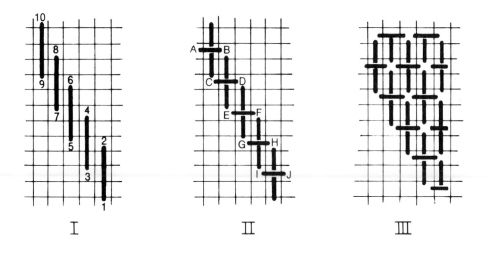

The Herringbone Stitch or the Plaited Stitch

The herringbone stitch is the head of a rather large family of related stitches, some of which don't even bear the family name, such as the plaited Gobelin, the velvet stitch, and the Bazar stitch. They all bear a family resemblance, however, either in the resulting stitch or the method used to achieve it. The basic stitch is a long stitch, slanted, with another long slanted stitch crossing it in the next stroke. All the stitches produce a rather tweedy texture except the velvet stitch which produces plush. They fit two thread canvas the best.

The herringbone stitch is a pleasant stitch to work on the larger mesh canvases; on the smaller meshes it is hard to see just where to put the needle. It is a fine rug stitch. It must be done from left to right only, not back and forth, or you will not produce the herringbone pattern. Work a row, finish off the thread, go back to the left side and start again.

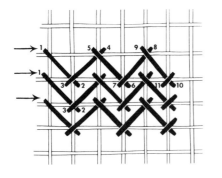

The Reverse Herringbone or the Herringbone Gone Wrong

This member of the herringbone family is more flexible than the previous one. It is worked exactly the same except that you can work back and forth this time, from left to right and then back right to left. The result is a pretty weave on the bias. This stitch is also done on the larger mesh canvases because it is easier to get the needle down between the stitches already done. Neither stitch carries much wool on the back of the canvas.

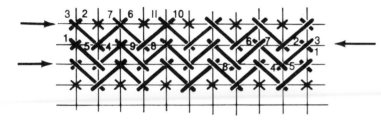

The Two-Color Herringbone Stitch

This stitch is primarily used as a rug stitch but it also works well on finer mesh canvas as a separate stripe or just in rows. The foundation stitches are done in one color and then the top stitches are worked over them in another color. Of course, it may be worked in one solid color. Be careful when working this stitch to keep your stitch tension even and a little loose. Because the row of mesh in the middle of the stitch stands empty it has a tendency to buckle or squash, thereby drawing up the canvas somewhat. Loose tension will prevent this. You may want to try a little more wool in the needle than usual to cover the canvas adequately.

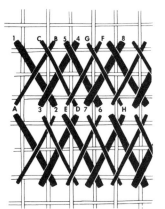

The Plaited Gobelin Stitch

The product of this stitch is a slightly more open herringbone running vertically instead of horizontally. It is worked in a different fashion from the regular herringbone but is still an easier stitch to work on large mesh canvas than fine mesh. It covers the canvas quickly and is rather fun to do. You will need to add extra wool to your needle to make this stitch cover the canvas.

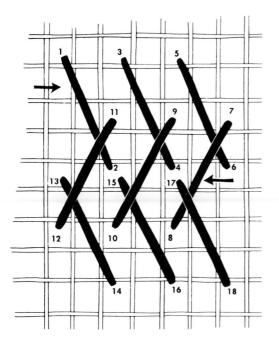

The Bazar Stitch or Six Color Herringbone Stitch

This stitch requires six journeys across the canvas to complete one row but it is worth it if you are looking for a highly decorative stitch. It should be worked on a two-thread canvas or leno canvas because it slips about on mono-canvas. The diagram shows how to start the stitch; when you have used up the four vertical mesh on which to start each row, start over again working down the vertical row. It is a very bulky stitch; you may wish to use less wool in the needle than usual. Work only from left to right. You will have to weave your wool into nearby canvas to start each row as there is little wool on the back of the canvas to help lash down. Keep your tension fairly loose to prevent the canvas underneath the stitch from buckling. Weave in any missing stitches at the beginning and the end of each row if necessary.

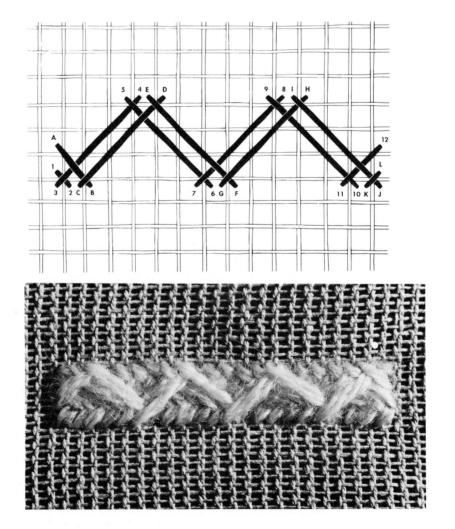

The Velvet Stitch or
the Closed Herringbone Stitch

For this stitch you'll need a little extra equipment, a strip of cardboard as long as your row of stitches will be and as wide as two mesh of the canvas you are using. This stitch is done over six mesh in height and is worked in three journeys over the same length of mesh, getting wider as one works. Work a row of herringbone stitch over two mesh of canvas using a strand less of wool than you intend to use on the outside or last row of herringbone. When completed place the long strip of cardboard over it on the face of the canvas. Work another row of herringbone over it, this time covering four mesh high with your stitches. Then work the final row of stitches six mesh high over the whole business.

On the back of the canvas, apply a coat of liquid latex such as Rug-Sta or Tri-Tix the length of the row. Allow it to dry. On the face of the canvas cut down as far as your guard strip of cardboard will allow, cut the length of the row exposing the cardboard. Remove it and hold the canvas near the steam from a tea kettle. This will make the wool fuzz nicely into a velvet-like nap. A leno or two-thread canvas is preferable over mono-canvas for this stitch.

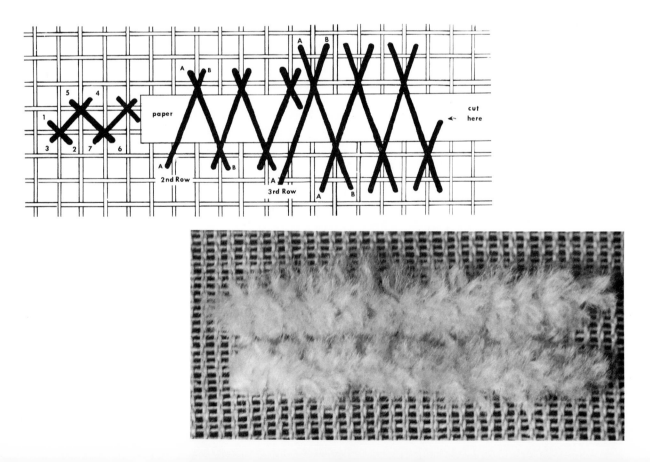

The Fern Stitch

The fern stitch makes a neat fat braid, it looks very much like a thick wale corduroy. It is quick and easy to work up and has a very thick backing. It must be worked from top to bottom only. If canvas shows between the rows either use more wool in the needle or work some little back stitches over the mesh to cover them. If you do the latter, a slightly different color gives a rather interesting effect.

1

New York Sky Line, pole screen worked in petit point. Designed and worked by Miss Lois K. Williams.

2

An American 18th century needlepoint picture worked with silk on linen. *Courtesy The Smithsonian Institution, Washington, D. C.*

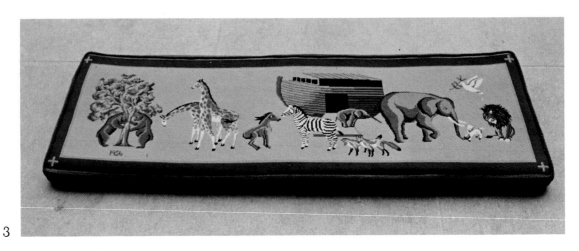

3

A kneeler from the Children's Chapel in the National Cathedral, Washington, D. C.

4

A marbleized paper pattern rug was designed and worked by Alexander Breckenridge of the New York School of Interior Design. The outside border with circles has various agate and stone patterns displayed, no two alike. There are over forty shades of green in the rug.

5

Needlepoint wall hanging originally of Danish design. Worked by Mrs. Barbara Miller Oeding of Australia who preferred to use her own colors and shading. The hanging measures nineteen inches by forty five inches.

6

The Three Graces, a Berlin work picture worked by Emma Frances Feather, aged 14, of Reading Pa., in 1855. *Courtesy The Smithsonian Institution, Washington, D. C.*

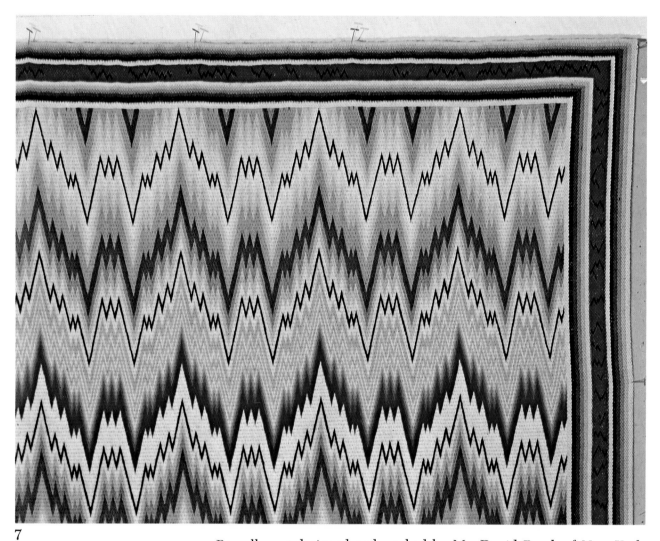

7

Bargello rug designed and worked by Mr. David Brush of New York.
The rug measures eleven feet, nine inches by seven feet, two inches.

Bargello wall hanging worked as an Embroiderers' Guild project by
Mrs. W. Glenn Deerey of Miami, Florida.

9

Unfinished needlepoint fan of 18th century Queen Anne style. English.
Courtesy Ginsburg and Levy, New York.

The Long and Short Oblique Stitch
or the Fishbone Stitch

This stitch is very similar to the previous one except that it looks a little lop-sided. It is just as attractive and as easy to do. Try doing the long stitch on one color and the short stitch in another color. In working the stitch one does all the long stitches first and then all of the short stitches.

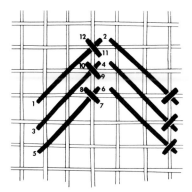

The Point de Tresse Stitch

If you want a super large braid this is the stitch to use. It can be worked on any canvas if the tension is loose enough. It is not as difficult to work as it looks. Try it as a border stitch or in stripes; it is too heavy looking for a background stitch. It is best to work the stitch as diagrammed rather than carrying the wool across the back, otherwise one has as bulky a braid on the back of the canvas as on the front. In the third diagram there ARE two stitches in holes 7 and 8. The first one got there as the last stitch in diagram one.

The Knotted Stitch

The knotted stitch is the first of a little group of tied down stitches which are worked in a similar fashion. They are all basically a long stitch or long stitches with a catch stitch in the middle. The knotted stitch takes strong hands to work, but it makes a tight snag-proof surface. It can be worked in two strokes of the needle without having to put your hand under the canvas. It is worked from right to left. It has one failing which is that it draws up the canvas from side to side. Over a large area this could make quite a serious problem if your canvas is to fit a certain space, such as a church altar kneeler or a card table cover.

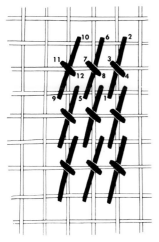

The French Stitch

The French stitch is the double tie-down stitch. It is a hard tight stitch and quite snag-proof. For a mass effect the French stitch looks neater than the rococo stitch. It works up slowly but does not pull the canvas out of shape. It has a firm backing. Be careful of your tension so that you don't cause the canvas to buckle.

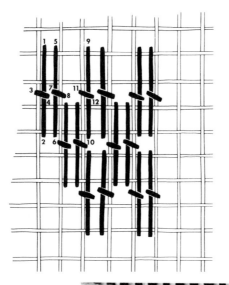

The Rococo Stitch

The Rococo stitch is one of our oldest popular stitches. It was a great favorite in the eighteenth century, both here and in England. This stitch is worked in diagonal rows. It can be used singly as a diagonal stripe on a field of half cross stitches or in rows as a backgrounding. This stitch is a terrible wool-eater.

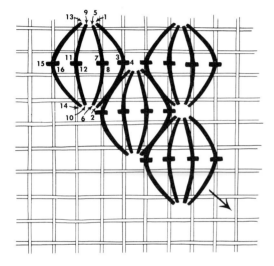

The Diagonal Shell Stitch

This stitch is the reverse of the Rococo stitch, four long stitches tied down by one. It has a thick bulky look and looks well on rugs. To cut down in the amount of wool on the back of the canvas it may be stitched in the fold way as shown in the diagram. This will also help prevent the canvas from "drawing up" thereby making that area of stitches shorter than the surrounding areas. It may be worked in vertical rows or diagonal rows but is easier to figure out worked vertically, at least until you are used to it. One must peek under the upright stitches to find where to bring the needle out to tie the stitch down. After a while you can do it by instinct. If canvas shows through at the top and bottom of the stitch, either add more wool to your needle or work a row of back stitches over the offending canvas. The stitch is quite adaptable to odd-shaped spaces since it can be halved.

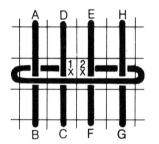

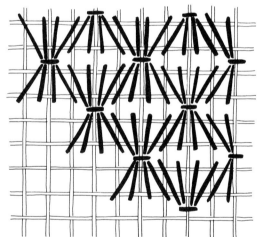

The Roumanian Stitch or the Janina Stitch

The Roumanian stitch was borrowed from crewel embroidery in the late nineteenth century and was renamed the Janina stitch. It is a very pretty member of the tied-down family but it has the bad habit of biasing the canvas. Working the stitch in a frame will control the tendency somewhat. It can be worked in two strokes on the surface of the canvas, and is worked from top to bottom. It does not look well in rows without an intervening stitch as the canvas peeks through.

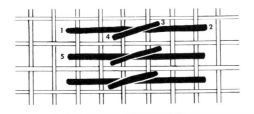

The Gobelin Stitch or the Upright Gobelin Stitch or the Straight Gobelin Stitch and the Renaissance Stitch

The Gobelin stitch is the first of a series of upright stitches, all based more or less on the same idea, a vertical stitch between the mesh. They all have the same traits. They cover the canvas quickly but are notorious wool eaters! The reasons for this latter trait are two-fold. In order to cover the canvas adequately it is necessary to add extra strands of wool to the needle. Then to make the stitches lie flat and straight, it is advisable to stitch so that there is as much wool on the back of the canvas as on the face. Wool does not like to bend, it prefers to coil. (See diagram.) Stitches that are not coil stitches will gap and lie "open" like the pages of an open book.

Try to keep the strand of wool untwisted as you work, the stitch looks neater untwisted and the wool is fatter when lying straight. It is very hard not to have canvas show between rows of the Gobelin stitch, however it combines nicely with alternating rows of any of the braid-like stitches such as the Greek stitch or the running cross stitch.

You can tramé this stitch and then it is called the Renaissance stitch. The tramé will beef it up and give it a pronounced ridge. Tramé unevenly along every other horizontal weft thread on mono-canvas, and between every pair of weft threads on penelope canvas.

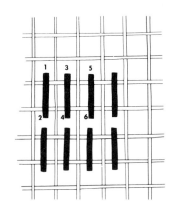

The Gobelin Stitch

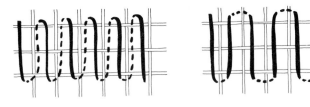

Wool coiling   Wool bending

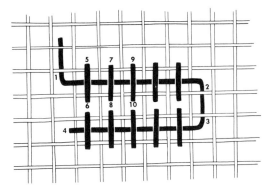

The Renaissance Stitch

The Gobelin Tramé Stitch

This stitch is a variation of the Gobelin stitch also. When it appeared in *Peterson's Magazine* in 1856 it was suggested that the tramé be done in braid, gold or silver, or straw. The key to success with this stitch is to have the tramé wool (or other thread) completely cover the two threads of mesh over which the upright Gobelin will be worked. You will have to experiment to achieve this. The tramé is worked row by row, just ahead of your Gobelin stitches. In this stitch, it is laid over an entire row of mesh, tucked into the canvas at the end of the row and then emerges for the next row of tramé. It is worked this way to keep the gaps of regular tramé from showing, which would spoil the woven look, and to keep the tension on the tramé thread loose enough.

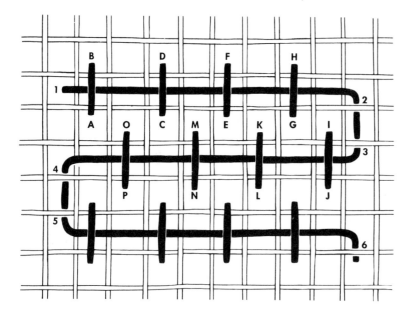

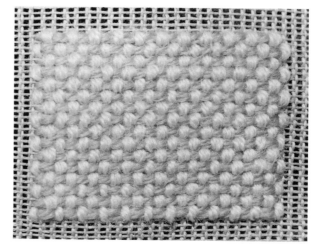

The Brick Stitch or the Alternating Stitch

The brick stitch is an excellent background stitch and is very easy to work. As with the other upright stitches you will have to experiment with your wool until you have added enough threads to cover the canvas. Use only leno canvas or mono-canvas for this stitch. Because two-thread canvases have too much space between their two threads, the upright brick stitch cannot spread out enough to cover the space. This is true of all of the upright stitches on two-thread canvases.

There are two ways to work the brick stitch. The first way is used just to cover the ground quickly. It is stitched diagonally so be careful your tension is even or a ridge of stitches will result. The first way is more economical with wool than the second way.

The second way is stitched horizontally, back and forth from left to right, and right to left. The canvas will bias if all the rows are worked from the same direction. The advantage of the second way is that it provides such a firm backing to the canvas. This is important if you are making a wall hanging or a rug and are using the basket weave stitch or some other heavily backed stitch. If a heavily backed stitch is worked next to a lightly backed stitch, the canvas will ripple in the lightly backed area. This will not block out. This would be most unfortunate on a rug border, for instance.

To give a clean edge to the stitch where it meets another kind of stitch, just work upright stitches over one mesh.

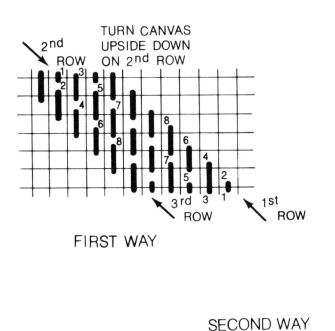

FIRST WAY

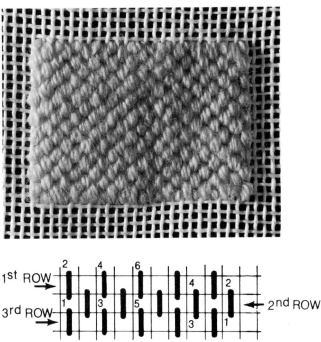

SECOND WAY

Bargello or the Florentine Stitch
or Florentine Embroidery or the Flame Stitch

Bargello as it is popularly called, is THE most popular stitch of all the fancy needlepoint stitches. It is also one of the oldest, having been used since the seventeenth century. It is a long upright stitch worked in "stair-step" patterns in progressive colors which repeat themselves to form a pattern. The most common count for a bargello stitch is four mesh high, with the next stitch occurring two mesh higher or lower on the canvas. This is called a four two step. Another combination could be six mesh high with the next stitch occurring two mesh lower or higher, this would be a six two step. The next row beneath follows the pattern set up by the first row. To show off the pattern each row is done in a different color or shade, with the sequence of colors repeating themselves down the canvas. This is what causes the flame-like appearance to the stitch. There are other variations, however, that are not flame-like but look like hearts, fish-scales, trees and diamonds. If the pattern is a peaked flame-like one, there is usually a center peak with the left side of the pattern being a mirror image of the right.

Set up your bargello canvas by folding it in half and running a basting thread up the fold. This will insure that the pattern will come out evenly on each side. With this stitch you count the HOLES between the mesh horizontally to plot the pattern across the canvas. Count the canvas threads vertically to figure the length of each stitch. Expect to use about a third more wool in your needle to cover the canvas. There should be no "lice" (a tapestry term) showing between the horizontal rows. If there is, add more wool to the needle until you get rid of them! Bargello should be worked only on mono-canvas or leno canvas.

It is important to twirl your needle to untwist the wool; the stitches should lie flat to cover and to look their best. The tension

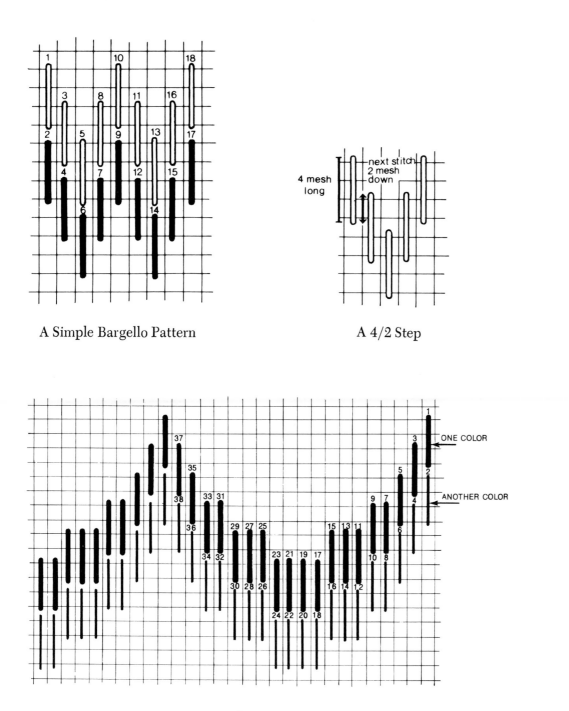

A Simple Bargello Pattern

A 4/2 Step

A Bargello wave pattern

should be fairly loose for this stitch; if your basket weave stitching is too tight, bargello will help you to loosen it up. As with the brick stitch, coil your stitches rather than bend them.

There are many excellent books available just on bargello patterns or try making up your own, which is really fun.

If you only have two-thread canvas or penelope, and you are eager to try bargello, try working a long cross stitch over the warp threads. Be sure you slant the top stitches in the same direction. You will be surprised how many people will think it is true bargello.

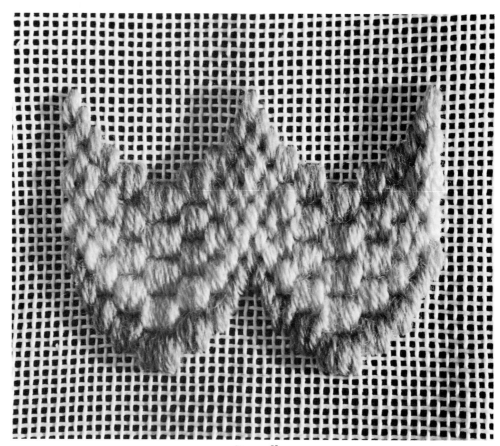

Bargello

The Old Florentine Stitch

This stitch is a set pattern stitch of the bargello type. It may be worked in just one color or in alternating rows of two or more colors. It is not very snag-proof in that the long stitches cover six mesh, but it does work up quickly for the same reason. Be sure that there is enough wool in your needle, about a third more than usual may be necessary.

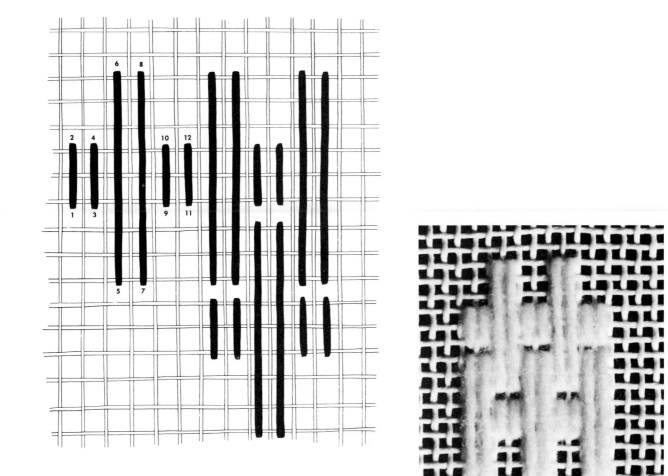

The Irish Stitch

The Irish stitch is an overgrown brick stitch and would be used the same way. It can be stitched the same ways the brick stitch is, and it too will require more wool in the needle to cover the canvas adequately. They look rather well together on the same piece of work. Make sure your wool is not twisted tightly as you stitch, each stitch should lie flat, fat, and even. Just twirl the needle in your fingers every few stitches, this will prevent it from twisting too much. The other thing to watch with this stitch is that your tension is loose enough to prevent the canvas from buckling or "taking up." Stitch a test swatch of a few square inches if it is important that the canvas not be foreshortened. If you find that your stitches draw up the canvas, work the Irish stitch in a frame.

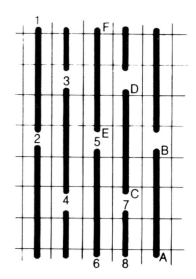

The Parisian Embroidery Stitch

This stitch has a close cousin, the Hungarian embroidery stitch, and they are hard to tell apart at first. They are both worked over two and four mesh but in different combinations; compare the diagrams and you will see. This cousin forms a stripe, while the other forms a diamond. This stitch looks equally well in one color or in alternating colors. More wool will be required to cover the canvas for both of these stitches. If you work it back and forth from right to left, then vice versa, the canvas is less apt to bias.

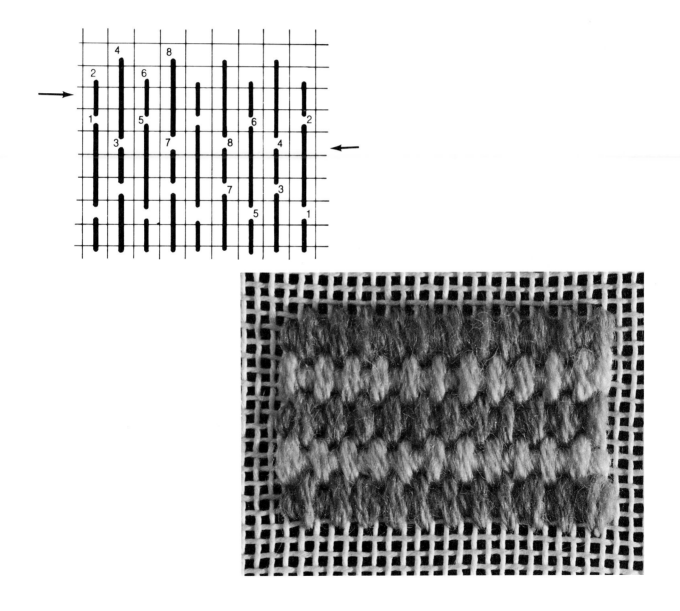

The Hungarian Embroidery Stitch

The Hungarian embroidery stitch is the trickier of the two related stitches, the other being the Parisian embroidery stitch. The reason for this is that one works three upright stitches to form the diamond and then a space is skipped before the next diamond is commenced. Once the pattern is set in the first row, the stitch becomes easier. This stitch is pretty done in two colors, it gives a diagonal checkerboard effect.

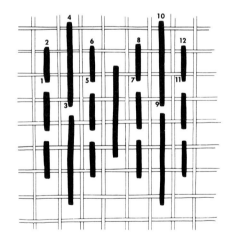

The Enlarged Parisian Embroidery Stitch

The enlarged Parisian embroidery stitch has a tie-down stitch which makes it less snag-prone than it would be otherwise with that long six mesh center stitch. The tie-down stitch, please note, is made from the same hole in the canvas, come up, go over the center stitch and then pop the needle back down the same hole from which you emerged. Worked over a large area this stitch does tend to bias the canvas, so a frame would be recommended. The stitch halves nicely which makes it more versatile for odd size spaces. You will need a third more wool in your needle for this stitch than you would for the half cross stitch on the same canvas. It has a very firm backing.

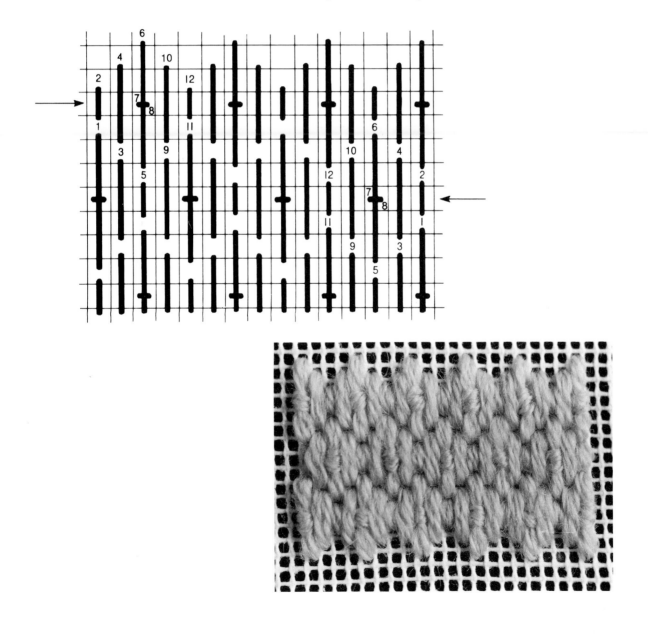

The Wicker Stitch

The wicker stitch looks like basket work. It can be used by itself for the pretty pattern or as an interesting texture stitch. It covers the canvas quickly and does not bias the canvas. Be consistent in the way you work this stitch; either coil the wool or bend it but not both on the same canvas. Bulges and ripples will be the result if you mix the stitch technique.

As you work each set of three stitches it is a good idea to hold back with your thumb the last stitch of the last set worked. This will expose more clearly the mesh that you will be working on next. To fill the gap that shows on the outside edge of a finished block of stitches, work a little row of half cross stitch or upright stitches over one mesh. Work this stitch only on mono-canvas or leno canvas.

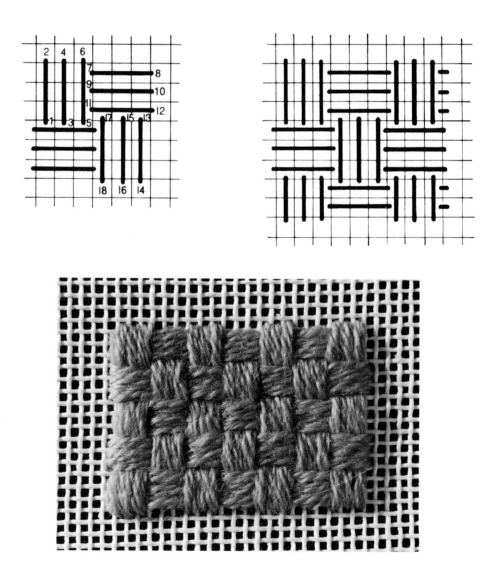

The Slanting Gobelin Stitch

The slanting Gobelin stitch is the simplest of all the slanting stitches. As a general rule the slanting stitches do not require extra wool in the needle to cover the canvas the way the upright stitches do. This stitch can be used over up to five horizontal threads or over two vertical threads as well as one. It has a very firm backing but will bias the canvas somewhat if worked over large areas. A frame is recommended.

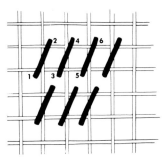

The Interlocking Gobelin Stitch or the Encroaching Gobelin Stitch

This stitch and the two following it are very much alike, they differ only in the way they are stroked or in the number of mesh they cover. The stem stitch in crewel embroidery is probably the original source.

The interlocking Gobelin stitch is a most attractive stitch, it works up quickly, makes a smooth hard surface on the face of the canvas and a nice thick back. However, it does bias the canvas and if you work your stitches tightly it will draw up the canvas. This means that the canvas will be shorter than you intended. Therefore if you are a tight stitcher, a frame is recommended.

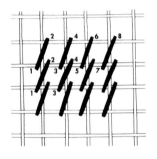

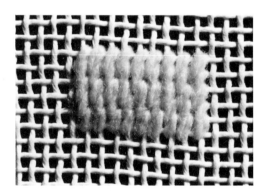

The Encroaching Oblique Stitch or the Soumak Stitch

This stitch may be worked vertically or horizontally whichever is more comfortable for you. It differs from the previous stitch in that it is stitched more like the stem stitch and not in horizontal rows. If worked in large amounts it will bias the canvas somewhat so a frame is recommended. It makes a rather nice background stitch if there are not too many small nooks and crannies it must be fitted into. At the beginning and end of each row work a two-mesh stitch to fill in the gap.

The Oblique Slav Stitch

The oblique Slav stitch is worked diagonally. If you will compare it to the encroaching oblique stitch you will see the similarity; this stitch is just two mesh higher. It is rather difficult to understand at first but quite simple to do once you catch on! The stitch works best with a fat amount of wool on a finer mesh canvas. Since there is not much wool on the back of the canvas it is fairly economical with wool. Its fault is that it is not very snag-proof. It may also be worked horizontally, as shown in the second diagram.

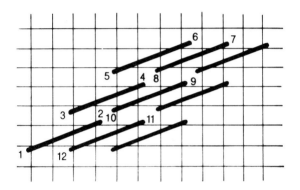

The Kalem Stitch or the Knit Stitch or the Knitting Stitch or the Reverse Tent Stitch

This is one of the best background stitches there is, it also does well for details in small areas, you can even outline in the stitch. For years rugs have been made in Greece using the knit stitch exclusively. It can be worked so that the texture runs vertically horizontally or if you choose, diagonally, see the following stitch description. If you look at the stitch closely you will see that it is really just the continental stitch worked wrong-side-to and in two different directions. The stitch does not bias the canvas very much because the different directions of the slant correct the tendency.

Work a half cross stitch at the beginning and end of each row slanting in the OPPOSITE direction than the row is to go. This will give a clean line to the edge of the stitch. This stitch takes just a little less wool than the half cross stitch would on the same canvas. It should be stroked in and out with one thrust on the surface of the canvas, however the canvas will have to be turned around and around as one must do with the continental stitch.

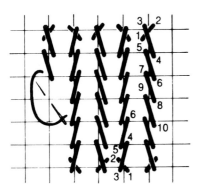

The Diagonal Knit Stitch

This companion to the knit stitch may be worked in either direction, just turn the book half way around to make it slant towards the left. One really has to think about this stitch to get the hang of it. In large amounts it will bias the canvas so a frame is recommended.

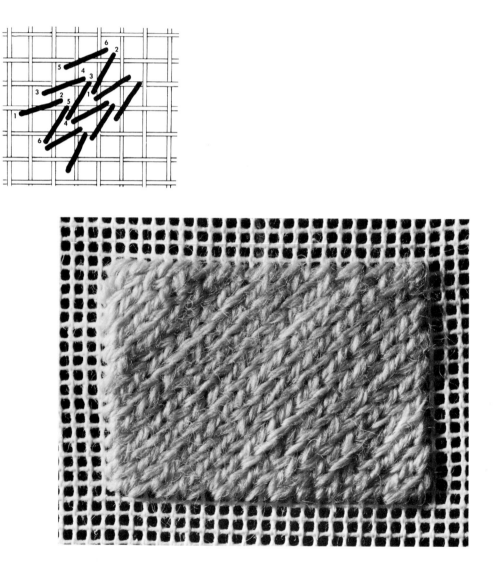

The Mosaic Stitch or the German Stitch

Here is another excellent background stitch, particularly if you are looking for a very small patterned stitch. It looks quite well as a border stitch also. It has a firm backing and will accommodate itself to any canvas. If you are going to be working very large areas of the mosaic stitch the canvas will bias if you stitch it tightly. In this case a frame would be recommended.

Working the stitch as diagrammed below will reduce the tendency to bias that will occur if you work each little "mosaic" separately. Work the small stitches first, basket weave style, and then work the long strokes in random horizontal or vertical rows. Do not work them in diagonally, this will increase the bias pull if you do.

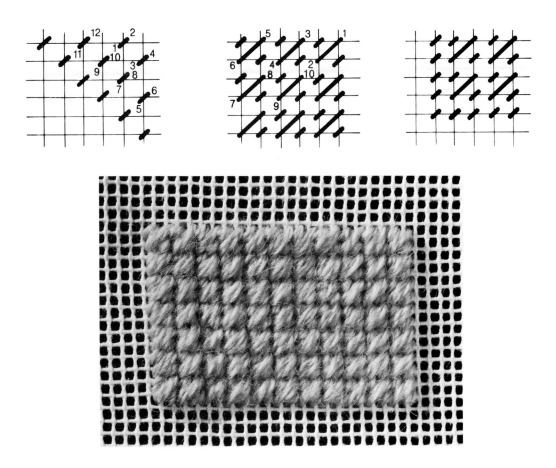

The Mosaic Stitch Done Diagonally or the Diagonal Florentine Stitch

This variation of the mosaic stitch makes a good background stitch also, but it does bias the canvas. A frame is strongly recommended. Try working it in alternating stripes using two colors. It is not too much of a wool eater.

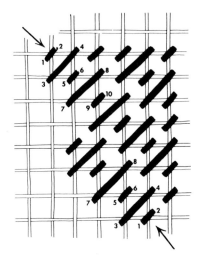

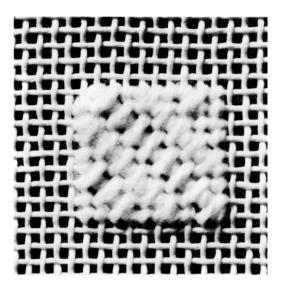

The Cashmere Stitch

The cashmere stitch has a neat embossed look about it, it makes a nice background stitch if you want a little pattern to it. It does not bias the canvas as much as the Scotch stitch but a frame would be recommended for large areas of it. It is rather fun to work, especially if you stitch it diagonally as shown in the diagram.

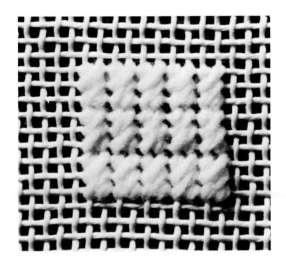

The Cashmere Stitch Worked Diagonally

If you happen to be looking for a stitch that looks like water ripples, this is the one. It is a nice stitch for other uses too, of course, but it is especially suited for water effects. It does bias the canvas somewhat, so for large areas use a frame. Work it diagonally as shown, or from right down to left.

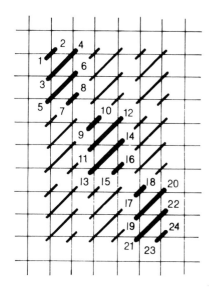

The Byzantine Stitch and the Jacquard Stitch

The Byzantine stitch is fairly easy to do once the first zigzag stripe is worked from top to bottom. After that you just follow the steps it made. The simplest way to do the stitch is from left to right. It does not pull the canvas out of shape as much as the other diagonal stitches. Try it in very strong colors.

The same stitch with a separating row of half cross stitch worked between each diagonal stripe is called the Jacquard stitch. Both stitches may be enlarged by adding more stitches on the horizontal and vertical steps.

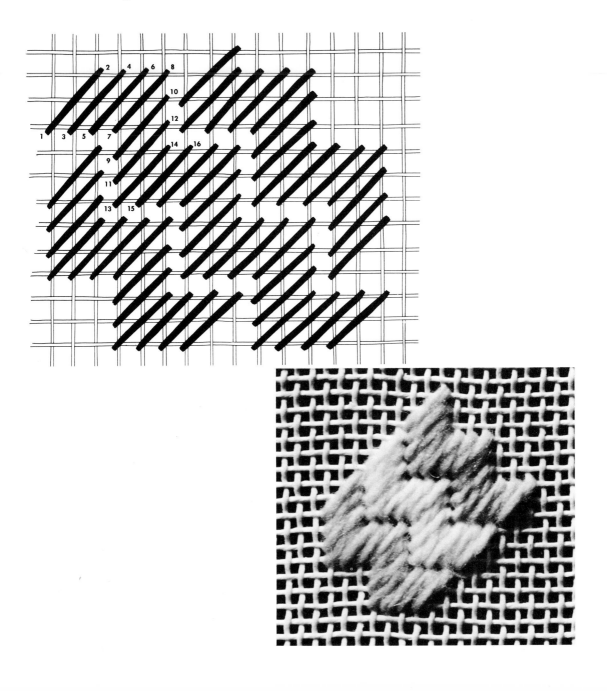

The Scotch Stitch and the Checker Stitch and the Point Russe Stitch

The Scotch stitch is a great favorite with needlepointers because it is attractive and versatile. It can be used by itself and in combination with other stitches to form interesting patterns. For instance, the Scotch square may be turned around so that it slants in four different directions, the whole thing can then be bordered with half cross stitch, or each square can be bordered with half cross stitch. The Point Russe stitch is a variation of the Scotch stitch using four halves of the stitch backed into each other and sometimes delineated by four long stitches. It is best used as a specimen stitch or alternately with squares of half cross stitch because when it is used as a grounding it looks just like a field of Scotch stitch unless every other stitch is a different color.

Alternating squares of half cross stitch with squares of Scotch stitch will form a checker-like pattern. This pattern is sometimes called the checker stitch. Another variation to make the stitch a little more snag-proof is to weave the needle over and under the stitch to create a woven effect. Always weave in the same direction, try using a weaving thread of a different color than the square itself.

If you work more than just a couple of rows of this stitch, an embroidery frame should be used. It is one of the greatest canvas biasers of all time. In addition to the frame, be sure you stitch with a slightly loose tension. You are literally tying the canvas into a slanted position as you stitch, and if it is stitched tightly there will be no hope of ever blocking it straight.

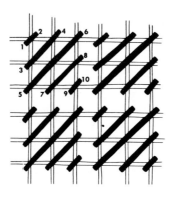

The Scotch Stitch

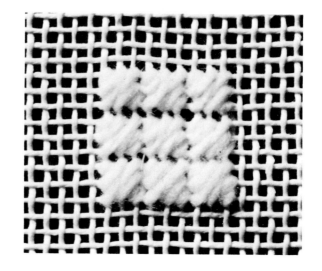

Variations on the Scotch Stitch

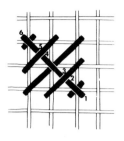

Woven Scotch Stitch

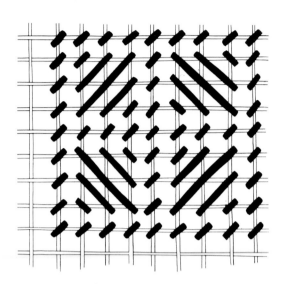

Scotch Stitch bordered with half cross stitches

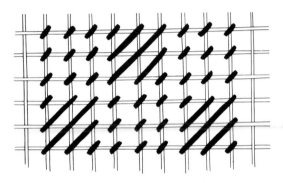

The Checker Stitch

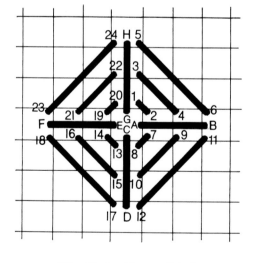

The Point Russe Stitch

The Scotch Stitch Worked Diagonally or the Diagonal Stitch and the Moorish Stitch

This stitch has a fat padded look to it, perhaps because it is almost padded. There is as much wool on the back of the canvas as on the front, furthermore a little more wool is needed in the needle in order to cover the canvas properly. The pattern does not lead the eye too strongly because the steps of the stitch are short. Like its parent stitch, it does bias the canvas and a frame should be used.

If a row of half cross stitch is worked between each diagonal row of the stepped stitches the stitch is called the Moorish stitch.

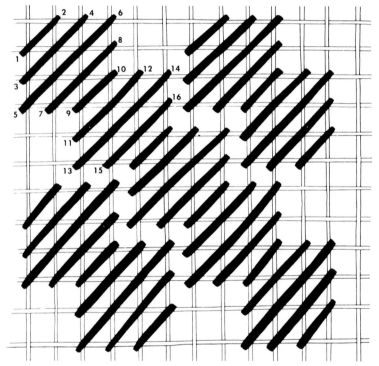

The Scotch Stitch worked diagonally

The Moorish Stitch

The Milanese Stitch and the Oriental Stitch

Another great canvas-biaser, the Milanese stitch enjoys great popularity because of the attractive pattern it forms. It is not very snag-proof either. Use a frame if you plan to work large areas of it. Working the stitch from the diagram below is rather like patting your head and rubbing your tummy, but it will cut down on the bias tendency. The stitch can be reduced in size and the effect retained by omitting that last long stitch and making it just three strokes long.

The oriental stitch is a variation of the Milanese stitch with a three stroke addition between each diagonal stripe of triangles. It is effective only if worked in two different colors.

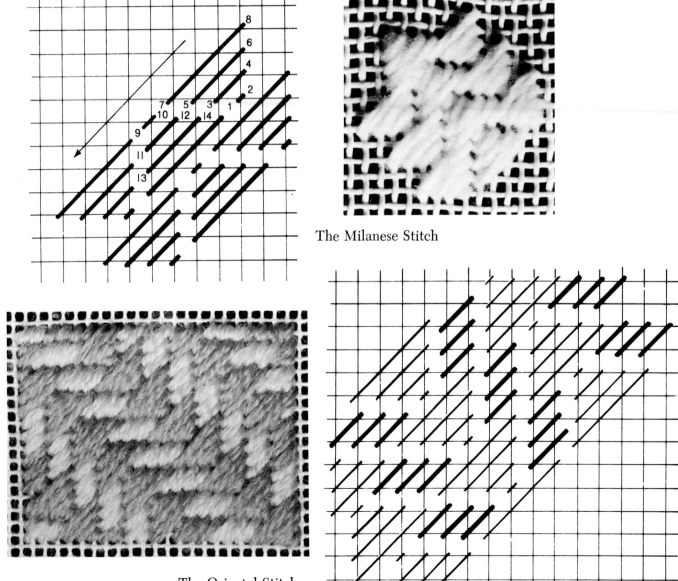

The Milanese Stitch

The Oriental Stitch

The Leaf Stitch

The leaf stitch is one of the most attractive and unusual of the fancy stitches. It is not particularly hard to do, has a nice backing and does not use an inordinate amount of wool. Its only drawback is that it is not very snag-proof as diagrammed. However, the stitch can be reduced as shown in the accompanying diagram. An upright stitch can be inserted on the leaf to resemble the main stem if desired. This stitch makes a very attractive border (see diagram) and is also handsome worked just by itself as a pillow or purse. You may have to use a little extra wool in your needle to cover the canvas.

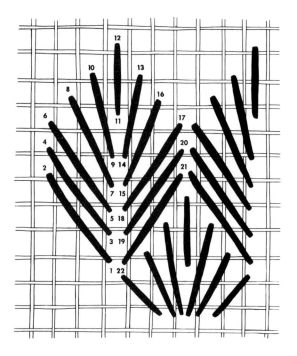

The Leaf Stitch

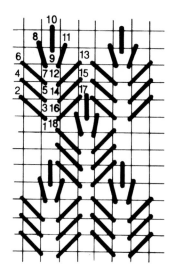

The Leaf Stitch modified

The Leaf Stitch used as a border

The Leaf Stitch modified

The Stem Stitch or the Long Oblique Stitch with Running Stitch and the Perspective Stitch

The stem stitch is another corduroy-like stitch, simple to do and with a fairly firm backing. It can be worked in two colors very effectively, the oblique stitches in one color, the running stitches in another. Use less wool in your needle for the running stitches than you do for the oblique. Put a half cross stitch at the beginning of each row, worked in the same direction as the following stitches, to close the little gap. Do the same at the end of each row.

The perspective stitch does not use the running stitch, just three pairs of oblique stitches overlapping three more pairs of oblique stitches heading in the opposite direction. This stitch may be worked in one color, but it needs two colors to show the "box" illusion of the stitch. The wool must fit the canvas exactly on this stitch or the canvas will show through in the center. Experiment until no canvas shows.

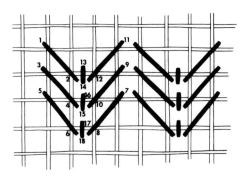

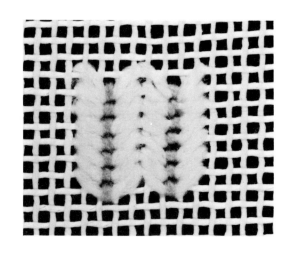

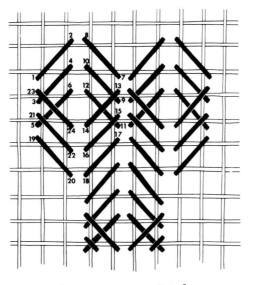

The Perspective Stitch

The Star Stitch or the Algerian Eye Stitch and the Eye Stitch and the Ray Stitch

The star stitch is the basic model of the following eight stitches. They are all ray or spoke stitches radiating out of one central mesh. They must be stitched very carefully or they will have a lumpy appearance. The star stitch is best worked on a two-thread canvas or a leno canvas. The stitch makes a flat square pattern. It is rather slow working up because you have to keep going back to the center mesh over and over. If the wool does not fit the canvas just right it will show through; however, you will find that you will need less wool rather than more. If the wool is too fat it is difficult to pull the needle through the same center mesh again and again.

If you enlarge the basic star stitch to four, six or even eight mesh the result is the eye stitch. It is difficult to work this stitch so that it has a neat appearance. The last stitch always seems to stand higher than the others.

The ray stitch is the eye stitch quartered. It should be worked over three mesh each way to have any definition at all. The rays may radiate all in the same direction or alternate, first to the right then to the left. The stitch covers the canvas best if the rays all radiate in the same direction. The ray stitch does bias the canvas somewhat.

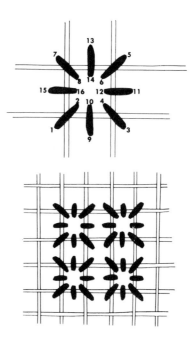

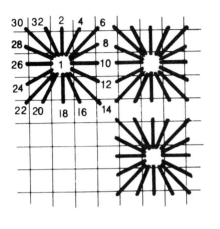

The Eye Stitch

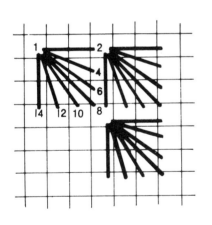

The Ray Stitch

The Diamond Eyelet Stitch

This stitch is another one where you must be careful to fit the wool just right to the canvas. If the wool is too thin the canvas will show through on the outer rays. Work the stitch in the same sequence for every diamond, a swirl effect is created and it should be consistent. On the diagram there are no odd numbers, they are all in the center at number 1. A running stitch may be used to outline the diamonds.

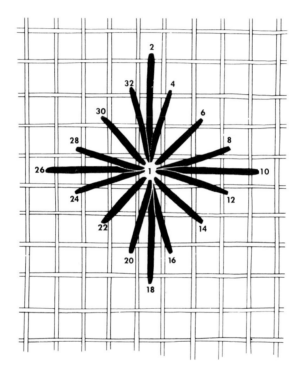

The Reverse Eyelet Stitch

This stitch must be combined with the half cross stitch to retain its identity. If it is worked in an all-over field it just looks like an eyelet stitch. The diagram shows the stitch plain, and then the lower right shows it quartered with a long stitch. The long stitch will cover up any "lice" showing through if the wool doesn't quite fit the canvas. You will need to work a square six half cross stitches by six half cross stitches to have the checker effect work out correctly.

The Triangle Stitch

The triangle stitch is a splashy geometric stitch. It is not very snag-proof but it does have a good firm backing. It cannot be used alone without the help of a cross stitch in each corner, otherwise there would be empty canvas there. Another way of filling this empty space is applicable if you are working a field of triangle stitches. Work all the triangle stitches, then fill those four four-mesh-by-four-mesh gaps with a double leviathan stitch. The triangle stitch sort of belongs to the upright stitch family, therefore it will not look well on a two thread or penelope canvas. You may need more wool in your needle to cover the canvas.

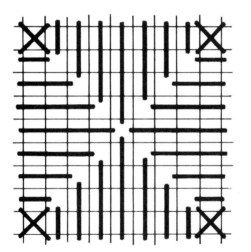

The Triple Leviathan Stitch

The triple leviathan stitch is a very decorative stitch that may be used by itself as a specimen stitch surrounded by half cross stitches or as an all over pattern stitch in horizontal rows. It shows itself off to best advantage on a fairly large mesh canvas. Try it in two colors, the rays in one color and the crosses in another color. Make sure all the crosses cross in the same direction. You may find that less wool in the needle will give a tidier look to the ray stitches.

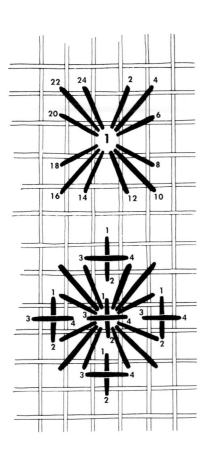

The Flower Stitch

The flower stitch can only be used as a specimen stitch; it cannot be used as a grounding stitch. It looks best if the half cross stitch surrounding it is worked in four different directions (see diagram). Work the outer stitches first, using a little less wool than you would ordinarily. Work the center cross stitches last, using the usual amount of wool. Then work the surrounding half cross stitches.

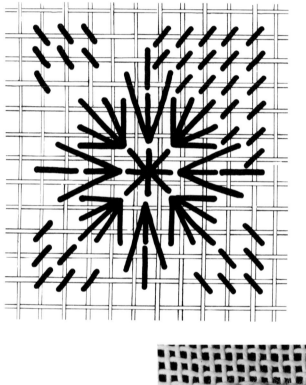

The Web Stitch

This stitch may best be described as tramé worked diagonally. The result does not look like needlepoint, it has a more woven appearance, very close and hard. It is advisable to do this stitch on a fairly large mesh for the sake of your eyesight. It works up very slowly, and therefore would never do as a background stitch because it is so tedious. It is mainly a special effects or accent stitch. Work a row of the diagonal tramé first, then cover it with the half cross stitches. Hold the canvas so that the tramé stitches are parallel to your body. You can follow the half cross stitch placement better that way.

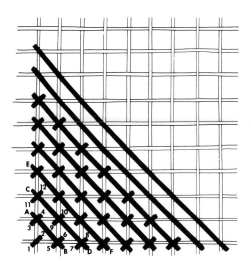

The Darning Stitch

The darning stitch is basically a rug stitch but with today's products it would be rather hard to work; rug wool is just too bulky. It fits a large mesh mono-canvas using tapestry wool much better. Persian wool is satisfactory too. You will have to experiment to see just what works best for you. The stitch is a great wool eater and is not very snag-proof. It is worked in four trips across the canvas using the same set of holes. Go over four canvas threads and under two to the end of your allotted space. On the return trip you will go over the canvas threads that you went under the last trip, and under the threads you went over. Make these journeys back and forth once more and the stitch is completed. The diagram shows on the right side how to handle an uneven number of mesh.

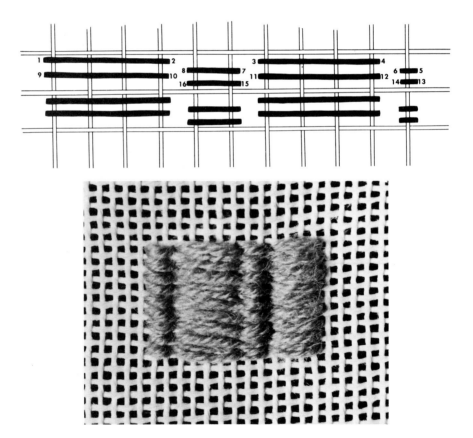

Turkey Work

Turkey work is the first of three shaggy and knotted stitches which are excellent rug stitches and are also wonderful accent stitches. They can be used to give a lion a mane, a doll hair, or a tail for a squirrel. This version, turkey work, can be worked on any canvas. On a two-thread canvas, a single stitch can be worked over one set of mesh to make a very dense pile. The stitch is usually worked over two threads of mono-canvas or leno canvas and over two sets of threads of two-thread canvas. To keep the turkey work pile from working its way into nearby stitches, complete all your other stitching before you start the turkey work. The space allotted for turkey work must be divisible by two, because each complete stitch uses two mesh. If you have one mesh over, work one surrey stitch there, it is the following stitch. No extra wool is needed in your needle for any of these pile stitches. Work the turkey work stitch from the bottom of the canvas up. It can be worked in either direction, right to left or left to right, whichever is the most comfortable for you. Use your thumb as the gauge to measure the pile and also to hold the wool down as you work the next stitch. Do not cut the pile until all the stitches are completed. Then trim with scissors. If you fear that small fingers will unpluck some pile, paint the back of the turkey work with a light coat of liquid latex. If you hold the cut pile over a steam kettle it will frizz nicely.

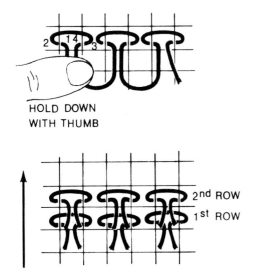

HOLD DOWN
WITH THUMB

2nd ROW
1st ROW

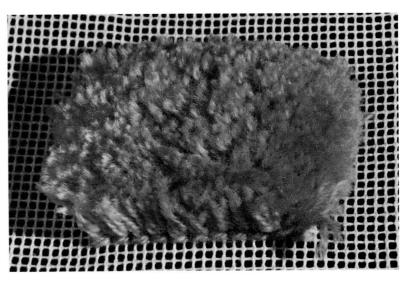

The Surrey Stitch

The surrey stitch is the same stroke pattern as turkey work; it is just done over an intersection of mesh instead of a pair of threads. The stitch slides about a bit on mono-canvas as it is being worked but is all right once the knot is pulled tight. The surrey stitch is also worked from the bottom of the canvas up. Don't cut the pile until you have completed all your stitches. The length of the pile should be about three quarters of an inch long before cutting. You can trim it or really mow it down shorter.

To start the stitch bring the needle in and out of the canvas as in diagram **a.** Holding down with your thumb the tag of wool left out, bring the needle and wool around to the left. Insert it from the right into the hole next door as in diagrams **b** and **c.** The needle must pass over its own tail, so to speak, to form the knot. To start the next stitch insert the needle at X as in diagram **d.** To start the next row begin in the row of mesh just above the row completed.

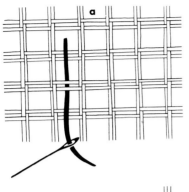

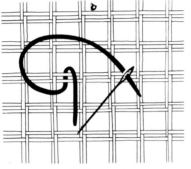

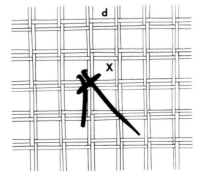

The Raised Work Stitch

This version of the plush stitch was popular in the nineteenth century. If you need just a row or two of a shaggy stitch this is the one to use. The other two versions, turkey work and the surrey stitch, are so much easier to stitch. This one is a little tedious, but does have a nice finished look to it because of the half cross stitch that locks it down. The half cross stitch also helps it to slant in one direction, perfect for a fringe.

You will probably need a little less wool in your needle than usual. It works most comfortably on leno or two-thread canvas. Start this stitch from the bottom of the canvas as you do for the other two, working from left to right up the canvas. Secure the loop or fringe with your non-needle wielding thumb as you work the locking half cross stitch. As with the other two plush stitches, this stitch should be the last stitch worked on the canvas. Work all the raised work stitches, then cut the loops open with your scissors. Trim to the length you desire. The steam from a teakettle will give a nice fuzzy look to the wool.

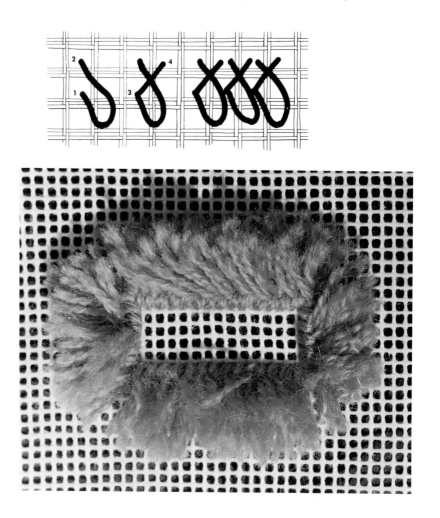

The Chain Stitch

The chain stitch does not look like needlepoint; it looks like knitting. Each stitch ties down the stitch before it. It takes some experimenting to get the wool to fit the canvas exactly, the problem being to have the wool thin enough not to crowd the mesh together as the stitch is worked. At the same time the wool must be fat enough to cover the canvas. Penelope canvas or two-thread canvas will accommodate this stitch better than mono-canvas. The chain stitch is worked from top to bottom only. Include the loop of the last stitch worked on each new stitch. Loop the wool under the needle to form the next stitch. To finish a row bring the needle up in the center of the last loop, and then down again over the next horizontal mesh. Run the needle through the backs of nearby stitches to anchor the wool. This means that at the end of each chain of stitches you must finish off the thread and then start fresh at the beginning of the next row.

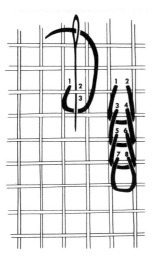

The Laced Chain Stitch

To start this stitch one must work a row of upright Gobelin stitch, work two stitches in every other mesh. For the next row, bring the needle to the surface of the canvas one row of mesh down and beneath an empty mesh. Pick up one Gobelin stitch from the pairs on either side of the empty mesh and then take the needle back through the hole you came up. Just remember that you always return to the hole you came out of and always pick up a part of two stitches above. You will probably need more wool in your needle to cover the canvas properly. To fill in the little gaps that occurred when you skipped every other mesh at the beginning, work a little upright stitch or two to cover. The diagrams show how to add or subtract a stitch. This stitch has very little backing and will not bias the canvas.

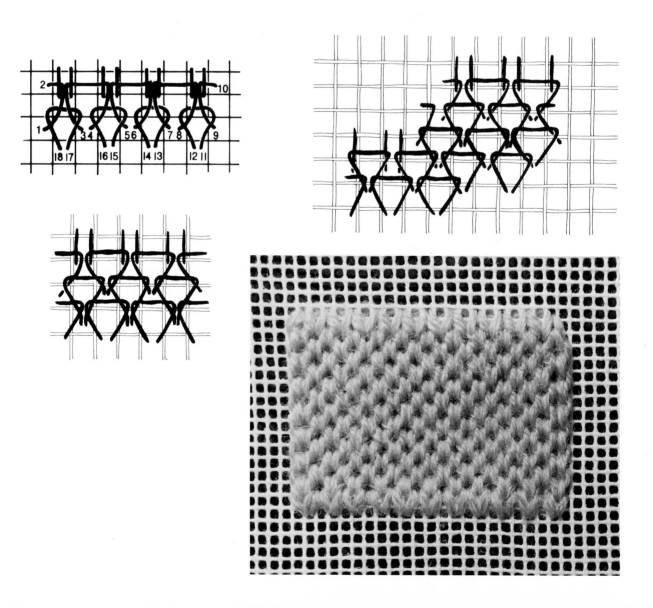

A variety of articles worked in needlepoint; belts, coasters, a zippered pouch, a billfold, knitting and handbags, man's slippers.

The amusing totebag was designed by Billie Conkling Needlepoint for Mrs. Edward R. Palmbaum of Baltimore, Maryland. The lion's body is worked in interlocking Gobelin stitch and his mane is composed of French knots. The waves rolling in on the beach on which he is sunbathing are made of slanting Gobelin stitch.

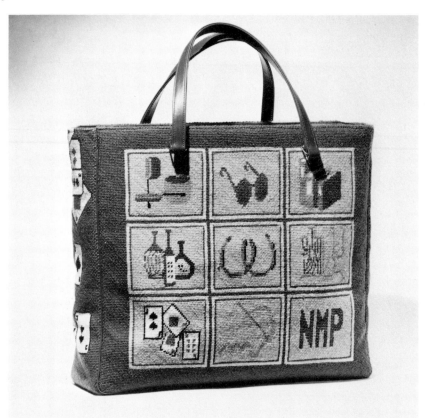

WAYS OF
JOINING CANVAS

XXXXXXXXXXXXXXXXXXXX XXXXXXXXXXXXXXXXXXXX XXX
XXXXXXXXXXXXXXXXXXXX XXXXXXXXXXXXXXXXXXX XXX

The Binding Stitch

The binding stitch is a finishing stitch and is important enough to deserve special mention. It is also known as the plaited edge stitch. It was originally used as a serging or covering for the selvages of one piece rugs. Now it is used as the decorative edging for glasses cases, bell pulls and tote bags as well as being used to join two pieces of canvas together. The stitch makes quite an enduring join as the wool passes through the canvas twice in the process of binding it together. The most important point to remember in the use of the binding stitch as a join is that the two pieces being joined must have an equal number of mesh to work over. The stitch forms a neat decorative braid which fits proportionately the canvas you are using. It is a reasonably malleable stitch in that it will turn corners and can be worked on a forty-five degree angle.

Whether it is used as a join or by itself, it is worked over the folded edge of the canvas, using two mesh for mono-canvas and just one set of mesh for leno and the two-thread canvases. Fold the canvas back four or five mesh or sets of mesh right next to your finished needlepoint stitches. Hold the work with the wrong side facing you. The binding stitch has a slight tilt, and the tilt will be facing the right side if held wrong side towards you. You may need just a little less wool in your needle than you would for the half cross stitch on the same canvas. The stitch is always worked from left to right. Fasten the wool in the backs of nearby stitches and with the needle pointing towards you, take a few stitches in the first mesh to make a good cover for the beginning of the braid. Take the needle over the edge of the canvas to the third mesh, through that mesh and back over the edge of the canvas to the first mesh again. Yes, it is the same mesh where you worked all those beginning stitches. Now forward and over the edge again to the fourth hole, and back and over to the second hole, forward and over the edge to the fifth hole and then back and over to the third hole. You always skip a mesh going backwards, that is, you don't go into the very next mesh going back, but the mesh after that. You always go into the next empty mesh going forward.

When you come to a corner, just mitre it (see diagram) and sail on around the corner, going back and forth as usual just as if the corner were not there. When you come to the end of a thread of wool, finish it off on a forward stitch. Run the needle into the backs of nearby stitches to fasten it down. Start the new thread very near the old thread by running the needle up through the backs of completed stitches, bringing it by the very hole the old thread just completed, then go on with your stitching just as if it were the old thread. When you finish the area you want to cover, just stop working the stitch any further forward and work in place, so to speak, for a stitch or two so that the braid will have a completed look; weave the tag end of the thread up into the finished braid.

If you are joining two pieces of canvas with the binding stitch, they must have the exact same number of mesh on each side. Hold the two pieces wrong sides together and match mesh for mesh. Proceed with the stitch just as if it were only one piece. This stitch will not join two pieces of canvas flatly, for instance as a rug join, but if you wish to join two pieces or edges of a glasses case or purse in a knife edge, the stitch works beautifully.

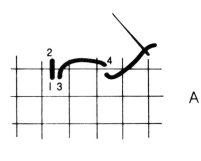

A

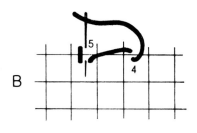

B

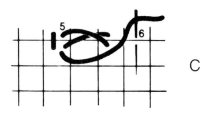

C

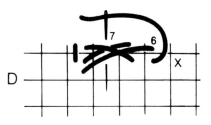

D

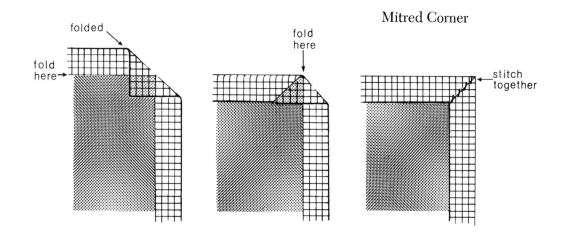

Mitred Corner

If you want you can prepare the canvas for the join while you are still in the designing stage, and before you have worked the canvas. You will need a spool of cotton thread for basting. Outline with chalk or crayon the design's outside border. Fold the canvas on these edges, counting on one set of mesh for two-thread canvas or leno canvas, and two mesh for mono-canvas. You will need five or six mesh or sets of mesh for a hem, cut the rest of the canvas away. Now fold the hem down and baste it. You want the two layers of canvas, the hem and the surface, to look as though they were just one layer of canvas. When you come to the actual needlepointing of this area you will treat it as if it *were* just one layer and stitch through both layers. Work the stitches right up to the folded mesh, then when the stitching is all completed, you will work the binding stitch over that folded mesh. Using this method you could pre-finish the sides of wall hangings, strip or one-piece rugs and bell pulls.

For a glasses case you would work the binding stitch around the mouth of the case after you have hand sewn the side seam on the wrong side of the canvas. Hand sew in the mesh in which are already the last row of needlepoint stitches. Match mesh for mesh and just back stitch the two sides together. Turn the case right side out and work the binding stitch around the mouth. Close the bottom of the case with the binding stitch, working through both layers and matching mesh for mesh. A pincushion could be made almost in the same way. Hand sew the side seam first this time, then close one end with the binding stitch, stuff it, and close the other end.

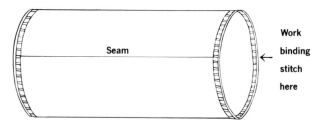

Seam

Work binding stitch here

The following joins may be used for rugs and other projects where the finished product will lie flat. The key to success in making any join of two pieces of canvas is that they are of the same type and mesh of canvas and ideally were cut from the same bolt. Each loom varies a little from the others so that the spacing of the warp threads can be just a little bit different, enough so that the mesh count will not be the same. If you are making a pieced rug, cut the rug pieces from the canvas as much as possible just as they will lie on the floor. This means that all warp threads will be going in the same direction. This is also true for church kneelers. After they are cut, crayon an arrow on each piece so that you can tell which way is "up." Numbering the pieces is an excellent idea too.

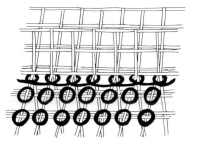

Joining two pieces of canvas, the seam sewn in the last row of worked stitches

The most simple join to do is to sew the two pieces of needlepoint together in the last row of worked stitches as suggested previously for the glasses case. This can be done by hand or machine, but by hand is better. Use very strong thread. Press the seam open and blind stitch the bare excess canvas to the backs of nearby stitches. Trim the canvas if the excess is more than one inch and a half.

A similar join works well with two-thread canvas. Pin the two pieces to be joined face to face, back stitch a seam between the two threads of the next set of mesh adjacent to your completed needlework. From the face of the work you will see that you have created a new set of mesh with your seam. Cover this new set of mesh with a

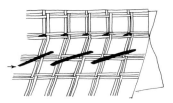

Joining two-thread canvas, forming a new mesh

row of quick point stitches in a matching wool. If you use this join with mono-canvas, work from the front of the canvas and whip stitch firmly the row of mesh nearest the needlework on each side. This forms one rather thick new mesh. Cover it with quick point.

Another variation of this join is to leave two rows of mesh bare of stitches nearest the work. Do this on each piece. Sew the third rows of mesh together, thus forming five rows of bare mesh, two from each side and the new one you created. Work the basket weave stitch or whatever stitch you were using over the bare mesh. The excess canvas on the back of the work should be laid flat and layered so that it appears to be one layer of canvas. Work through both layers. Then trim the excess canvas away to within three-quarters of an inch of the join, after the join has been completed, however. This is a very secure join, but it must be planned for in your design, otherwise you will have an odd blank stripe of color where the join is. It is not a bad idea to paint the raw canvas edges with liquid latex to prevent ravelling.

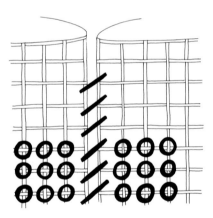

Joining mono-canvas, forming a new mesh

Canvas is joined, then stitches are worked over five-mesh strip

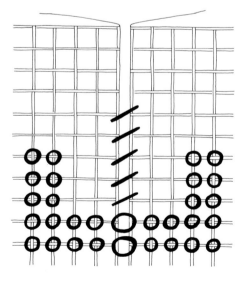

ANOTHER VERY SIMPLE JOIN is just placing one edge of the canvas over the edge of the other piece. Again they are layered so that it appears that they are just one piece of canvas. The stitches are worked through both layers, and the layers need only overlap about an inch. The only trouble with this join is that the cut edge of canvas on the top has a tendency to poke its way through the stitches showing a canvasy stubble. You can cover the stubble with a nice bulky stitch such as the double leviathan stitch or the Smyrna cross stitch. If you can plan your join so that a row of such a stitch would be appropriate then you have a very easy job ahead of you. It will be even easier if the join were near a border where several rows of the bulky stitch would be fitting. It is a good idea to paint the cut canvas edges with liquid latex to prevent ravelling.

To join four pieces of canvas, sew them together in pairs first. Use good stout carpet thread and stitch in the last row of completed stitches. Match mesh for mesh. When both pairs are joined then join the pairs. Somehow it seems easier if you start this seam from the very center of the joins and work towards the edges. When you have joined all four pieces together, make a cross stitch with wool and from the back of the canvas, in the very center of the join, picking up canvas from diagonally opposing sides. This cross stitch is made to avoid having a tiny hole right in the center of the join. Mitre the corners (see diagram) of each piece of canvas after the join is made to make the canvas square up sharply.

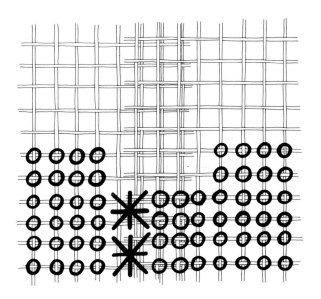

Cut edge laid over cut edge with Smyrna cross stitch covering the edge

"The Queen of Sheba Admiring the Wisdom of Solomon" is the title of the
petit point picture which was made in Massachusetts in 1774. Note the
fiddler on the right of the tent and the man with his tankard of ale on the
left. *The Smithsonian Institution, Washington, D.C.*

Needlepoint rug designed by the Women's Home Industries Tapestry Shop in London, England. Worked by Mrs. Barbara Miller Oeding of Strathfield, New South Wales, Australia. Mrs. Oeding substituted the Siamese cat square of her own design. The rug is seven by four feet.

11 A raised work picture worked on wool with wool in the mid-nineteenth century. The bird has been trimmed with scissors to give it the sculpted effect. *Courtesy The Smithsonian Institution, Washington, D. C.*

17

This interesting sampler tote bag was designed and worked by Mrs. Charles Hellman of Hastings-on-Hudson, New York. The geometric pattern is a very old one but its treatment here gives it a very contemporary flavor.

Dampen the canvas by either sponging it with cold water, spraying it, or, if the piece is quite biased, rolling it up in a wet towel as you would a sweater. Let it absorb for six or eight hours before checking to see if it is damp enough. If you totally immerse a canvas you will remove most of the sizing and possibly encourage any non-fast dyes or paints to run. If there are fancy textured stitches on the canvas, block it face up, otherwise it doesn't really matter whether it is face up or down.

Before laying it out on the board, pull and stretch it back into some sort of shape. Pull in the opposite direction of the bias and use a fair amount of muscle. Tack the canvas down on the canvas, a preliminary tack in each corner about half an inch away from the finished work. Place the tacks in the holes of the canvas, not through the threads. Then with an even tension, tack between each corner and so on, quartering and re-quartering around the canvas, tugging every now and then to make the canvas straight and true. At the same time, try to line up the needlework with the T square which you can brace on the sides of the board. If you place the T square right over the edge of the work, it is easy to tack into the adjacent canvas. Work round and round until you are satisfied that the canvas lines up quite straight. You may have to remove and replace a few tacks. There may be a tack every half inch before you are through, perhaps less. It will take about twenty-four hours for the canvas to dry. When blocking a circular canvas, treat it as if it were square as far as the tacking is concerned. At the same time you must try to ease it into its proper circular shape.

If the canvas is hardly biased at all, use just a hot iron and a pressing cloth on it. The steam created loosens the canvas a little, you can give it a tug or two and then just let it dry on the ironing board for an hour or so.

The larger figures are worked with silk on canvas and applied to a white satin ground worked with metal threads. English mid-17th century. *The Metropolitan Museum of Art, Rogers Fund, 1913.*

A true bargello chair seat, one of a set. *Courtesy, Mrs. Thomas P. Dillon and worked by her mother, Mrs. Edith Pratt Maxwell.*

Mounting

There are few things that you cannot mount yourself. Large upholstered furniture, chair backs and arms, and leather-trimmed handbags are, of course, best done by professionals. Pillows, stools, slip seats, clutch bags, kneelers and pictures can be done at home. The most obvious advantage is economic. Professional mounting is usually very expensive.

Slip Seats   When your seat cover is finished and stretched you should have an inch to a half inch more finished work all the way around the seat than you need. Place the canvas just the way you want it on the chair seat and stab through it with straight pins in the four corners and the center. This will help hold it in place while you are working on the back. Gently turn the canvas and seat over, bottom side up. With someone helping you, pull the canvas tight front and back and tack it. The tacks should go one half inch in from the edge. Pull the canvas tight from side to side and tack it. Fold the excess canvas over in the corners, pull it firmly and tack it in opposing corners. That is, tack one corner, then the one opposite, then the last two. If there is a lot of curve to the seat you will have to take little tucks in the canvas as you work around. Work your way around the canvas from side to side stretching *evenly* as you go. Turn the whole thing over occasionally to make sure you are not stretching unevenly. When you are finished you should have a tack about every inch or so. Trim the ruffle of canvas left, one-half inch from the tacks will do. Cover the bottom of the seat with black or white muslin using fewer tacks and placing them closer to the edge of the seat. Stretch the muslin taut, but not tight.

Pillows   Pillows look best with some cording or fringe at the edge. Commercial fringe looks very nice if you can match the color. You can make your own cording by cutting enough bias to go around the pillow from the material you are using to cover the back of the pillow. Fold the bias over common household cord and sew it as close as the sewing machine foot will allow. Sew your cording, cord side in, raw edge side out, on to the very edge of your finished canvas. Shaping is required when turning corners with the cording. Baste the pillow backing (right sides facing each other with the cording coming in between) right along the seam of the cording. Machine stitch the canvas, cording and backing together, following the basting stitches and leaving an end open to reverse the cover and to insert the pillow. Hand stitch the opening together as close to the cording seam as possible. The fringe can be handled the same way as the cording, the fringe will be facing in when you attach it to the worked canvas. Don't forget to shape the corners a little with the fringe too.

Clutch Bag   Do a piece of needlepoint 20 inches by 8 inches. (Your sampler?) When it is stretched, cut a piece of lining material an inch larger all around than your worked piece. Mount a zipper to the narrow ends of the needlepoint piece so that you have a large ring or muff of needlepoint and zipper. With the wrong side out sew the lengthwise seams of the needlepoint. The zipper will be in the middle of the purse, giving a saddle-bag-like pocket on each side of the zipper. Sew the seam right on the edge of the last worked stitch. Trim off the excess canvas within a half inch of the seam, trim the corners of excess bulk. Turn it right side out through the zipper opening.

Again with the wrong side out sew the sides of the lining material together so that you have a saddle-bag arrangement with a half inch of material separating each bag. Trim the seams of the lining and insert into the needlepoint envelope just the way it is. Stitch the lining to the zipper seam by hand on each side, and stitch the edges of the center of the lining to the zipper ends. Press with a damp cloth.

Foot Stools   The important thing with foot stools is to make sure the finished work really fits the stool. Assuming that your stool cover has boxed corners, trim the excess canvas to within an inch all around and to within a half inch in the corners. Hem up the bare canvas to the back of the worked canvas with a basting stitch. Bring the corners together, then oversew them together with matching wool from the outside, or you can machine a seam from the wrong side. Oversewing from the outside insures that no bare canvas will shine through. Trim the corners of excess bulk. With upholstery tacks nail the needlepoint to the stool (with or without gimp). This is a two-man job. You will need someone to hold it in place as you work back and forth and from side to side.

A Victorian cricket stool with the diaper pattern covering is one of a pair; they were made from the tops of piano stools and the remains of the screw is still in the underside of each stool. *Courtesy, Mrs. Thomas P. Dillon.*

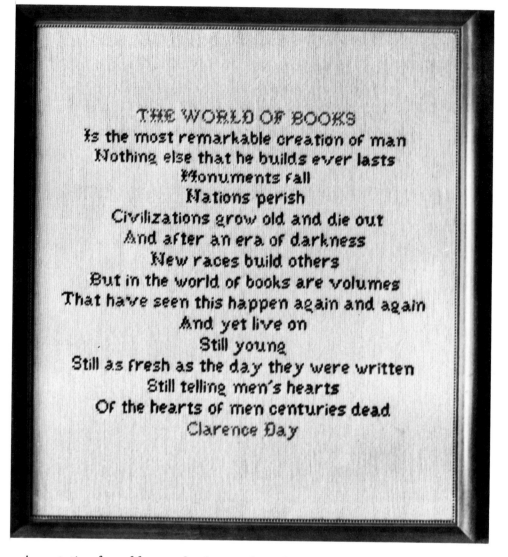

THE WORLD OF BOOKS
Is the most remarkable creation of man
Nothing else that he builds ever lasts
Monuments fall
Nations perish
Civilizations grow old and die out
And after an era of darkness
New races build others
But in the world of books are volumes
That have seen this happen again and again
And yet live on
Still young
Still as fresh as the day they were written
Still telling men's hearts
Of the hearts of men centuries dead
Clarence Day

A quotation for a library; the frame, the title, and the name are in a warm rose color, the rest is in black and white. *Courtesy, Dr. Henry L. Darner.*

Mounting a Picture   Stretch your canvas as true as you can. Cut a piece of cardboard one stitch smaller than your finished picture. The cardboard used in gift boxes is an excellent weight to use. Trim the excess canvas from your picture, leaving a generous inch on all sides and a generous half inch on the corners. Place the cardboard on the wrong side of the canvas. With carpet thread and needle handy, fold

A view of the Crystal Palace, London, site of The Great Exhibition of 1851, worked in silk and wool. *Cooper-Hewitt Museum of Design, New York.*

back that half inch of bare canvas right to the corner stitch. Sew the folded edges together. Do this to the opposite corner next, and then the remaining two corners.

If the picture is more than six inches across, lace the excess canvas from top to bottom, and from right to left with the carpet thread. Press each corner on the wrong side as hard as you can. You want the back of the picture to take up as little room as possible in the frame. If you are not having a framer go on from there, order a frame the exact measurement of your mounted canvas. Try to choose one that will be deep enough to hold the bulk. Vacuum-clean the canvas before you lay it in the frame, lay a piece of cardboard in on top and tack it with the nails provided, first in the center of each side and then a few nails close to the corners. Cut out a piece of brown paper just a quarter of an inch smaller than the frame edge. Glue this with a good stout glue to the back of the cardboard and the back edge of the frame. This paper cover will keep the dust out.

The design on this pillow was adapted from a Hiroshige woodblock by Gladys B. Schmidt of Bethesda, Maryland, for Mrs. Bennett Olshaker of Washington, D.C. The colors are quite true to the original woodblock.

ET CETERA

Picking Out Mistakes   You need two things to pick out mistakes, a pair of sharp-nosed sewing scissors and a very light touch. Insert the tip of the scissor under the wool a stitch at a time, take it slow and easy, so as not to cut the canvas. Snip in the direction that you stitched. When you have snipped all the stitches that you need to, put away the scissors and pick out the stitches with a needle until you have reached the end of that thread or have enough to put in the needle to finish off in the back of the canvas. You will have to snip both front and back and then pick out your "snippage" with your fingernails. It is slow, delicate work but worth it to get rid of a mistake.

Strengthening a Weak Spot   The reasons for strengthening would be a weak split thread, or a cut thread from careless stitch removal. Cut a piece of matching canvas one-half inch larger than the area that needs strengthening. Loosely baste the patch to the wrong side of the canvas with a piece of wool. Match up the mesh as carefully as you can. Stitch right over the canvas, going through the patch's mesh too, just as though the patch were not there. When that area is completed, trim any canvas threads poking out from the back. If you have one cut thread, ravel a thread from the edge of the canvas to serve as a patch.

155

Lay it under the cut thread. Touch the cut ends with a drop of liquid latex and also the ravelled thread. Hold them all together for a few minutes. You want the cut ends to bond and the reinforcing thread to adhere to them. When the patch is dry, trim the ravelled reinforcing thread to about an inch from the patch on each side. Gently work your stitches over and around the patch.

Applique

There are two reasons for appliquéing one piece of canvas to another: to give greater detail to one area such as the face of a figure or the petals of a flower; and to allow more than one person to work on a large project. An example of the latter is the War Memorial tapestry in the Washington Cathedral in Washington, D. C. The tapestry measures 9 by 12 feet. The large background pieces (sewn together when completed) showing the branches of a tree were worked by one group of individuals and the state seals which are appliquéed to the branches of the tree were worked by other individuals. The seals were tied in.

Appliqué is generally done on mono-canvas since the same idea may be achieved on penelope by just separating the mesh and using petit point for the details. However, on some old canvases penelope was used for the gros point and petit point and then gauze was appliquéed to give even greater detail.

If you are appliquéing two pieces of the same mesh canvas the appliqué piece must be the exact mesh count as the blank space it will fill. Thus a piece which is fourteen mesh by twelve mesh will fit into a blank space fourteen mesh by twelve mesh. If the mesh of the two pieces of canvas do not match you must rely on exact linear measurement. Make sure that all the stitches of the appliqué will be going in the same direction as the background canvas.

Detail of the War Memorial tapestry. A large tree bears the seals of the fifty states. The emblems of the five services have also been worked into the design. Each state seal was appliquéed by the tying-in method onto the background canvas. *The National Cathedral, Washington, D.C.*

The Sew-on Method of Appliqué   Block the pieces before sewing them together. If the piece to be appliquéed is large enough machine stitch with fine thread around the very edge of the worked area. The pieces must fit exactly. Trim the edge of the appliqué to a quarter of an inch from the worked area. With a single thread of silk, or matching cotton thread, stitch the excess quarter of an inch to the back of the worked area, allowing no stitches to show through to the front. Mitre sharp corners if necessary. With a single thread of silk, baste the piece lightly into place. Using a single thread of the same color that edges the appliqué, blind stitch the appliqué to the canvas. Your needle will be going through worked appliqué to bare canvas, your fingernails will help in holding the piece into place. Sometimes the threads of the canvas or gauze of the appliquéed piece poke through the worked area to the front. There is nothing that you can do to prevent this without adding bulk to the appliqué.

The Tie-in Method   This is the method to use for pieces of canvas of the same mesh, of no more than four mesh difference. Tying in pieces that have a difference of more than four mesh produces botchy looking appliqué. The piece to be appliquéed must have a border of at least two inches of unworked canvas on all sides. Unravel the bare canvas border. When unravelled the piece will have a fringe of canvas threads around it similar to the fringe on a rug. Using a short blunt needle, thread one of the canvas fringes into the background canvas. Put the needle into the nearest completed stitch hole, pull the thread through, free the needle and go to the very next canvas thread and thread it into the background canvas. Do about an inch this way and then stop to tie the canvas threads together by pairs. If the mesh are not the same you will have to draw two threads through one hole in some places, space them evenly. Don't pull too hard on the individual canvas threads or they will pull right through and out of the canvas all together! Press with a damp cloth or steam iron when finished. If the canvases are not too stretched out of shape before appliquéing they may be blocked after appliquéing.

Canvas unraveled in preparation for tying-in to background canvas.

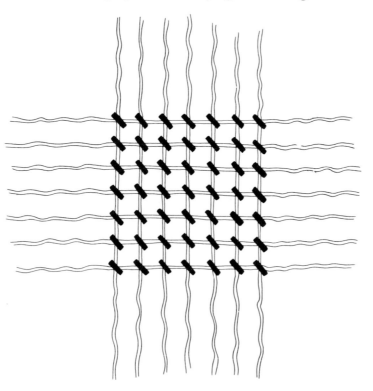

A small stitch sampler stretched.

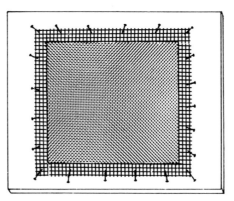

The shepherdess and her dog are petit point, her face and arms were done on gauze and then appliquéed on. *Courtesy, Mrs. Roman V. Mrozinski.*

Detail of the shepherdess showing the gauze appliqué, the petit point and the gros point. She wears a hair ribbon worked in silk. Her eyelashes and eyebrows were embroidered in over the half cross stitches.

The altar frontal, "Feed My Sheep" will be mounted on velvet and bound with gold cording when completed. It was worked by Mrs. Elizabeth Rollings and was designed by Ann Oster of Billie Conklin Needlepoint in Baltimore. The French knotted sheep are resting in a field of darning stitch.

RUGS

Rugs are a great joy to make, they give one such a sense of accomplishment and are so useful. If you are a real needlepoint addict and are tired of making pillows and pictures, take the plunge and try a rug! A simple one-piece strip rug is a good way to start. For your first attempt use a fairly large mesh canvas or it will seem that you are working on it forever. Ten mesh mono-canvas is about as fine as you would want, seven mesh penelope is a good rug quality and then of course, there are the five mesh two-thread rug canvases to choose from. Seek advice from your favorite shop on just what wool to use with each canvas. The availability of wools in your particular area is one consideration, and what covers the canvas to your taste is the other consideration. Fancy stitches lend themselves to rug use particularly well. Some favorites are the cross stitch, the double cross stitch, the Greek stitch, the Kalem stitch, any of the herringbone family and the Smyrna cross stitch. Any of the tufted stitches are suitable too.

Currently, canvas is about forty inches wide. You can work it either warp-wise or weft-wise except on penelope canvas. This gives you a choice of a rug with the selvages on the ends and perhaps thirty inches wide, or a rug with the selvages on the sides, forty inches wide and perhaps sixty inches wide. Your design, the scale of the design and canvas and the location of the finished rug will help you make your decision.

To start a rug on any canvas, in either direction, fold back about two inches of canvas on the cut ends and match up the layered mesh. Baste the hem back. Work your stitches right through the hem as if it were just one layer of canvas. Treat the other side or end the same way.

Using a frame for your rug will really guarantee that it will not bias and will always lie straight and true on the floor. Work the first few rows of your rug through the basted hem and then pin or sew the worked hem to the tape attached to your rug frame. If you decide on the forty-inch wide rug you may have to use a rug hooker's frame which is very similar to an embroidery frame. If your frame has no tape, use aluminum tacks to tack it to the cross bars. Attach the other end of the rug to the other cross bar and wind up the rug on the cross bars until you have a nice tight surface on which to work. Lash the sides of the rug to the sides of the frame with carpet thread and you are ready to work. Work the binding stitch over the selvages when you finished. You can work the binding stitch on the hemmed sides or ends or make fringe. To make the fringe, cut your wool into six-inch pieces. With a crochet hook inserted through the canvas at the bottom row of mesh, catch the middle of the six inch piece of wool and pull it through the canvas enough to make a loop. Pull the two dangling ends of the wool through the loop and pull it tight. Trim the fringe to even it off when you have finished.

A strip rug can be blocked just as you would a pillow or any other piece of needlepoint. One needs an old door or a floor on which you don't mind making a few tack holes; attic floors are just right. Lay down a layer of brown paper; dampen the rug with a sponge or spray; place the rug on the paper and stretch it as you would a smaller canvas. Obviously this is a two man job, and obviously the T square won't work on the floor. You will have to line up the sides of the rug with the sides of the paper or with lines that you have crayoned on with the aid of a yardstick. You will probably have little blocking to do, especially if the rug was worked in a frame.

If you feel a lining is necessary for your rug, use a very even weave material such as linen or herculon. If possible it should be pre-shrunk. Lay the needlepoint face down on a table, then the lining on top of that and face up. Working from the center, pin the pieces together so that they will lie smoothly and evenly. Fold back the lining so that it is even with the edge of the canvas, then blind stitch the lining to the needlepoint, picking up with your needle on each stitch a little canvas and wool. You will be stitching into the last row of needlepoint stitches. Stitch the long sides first and then the ends.

A cushion cover worked in wool, "The Prodigal Son Leaving His Parents," English early 17th century. *Cooper-Hewitt Museum of Design, New York.*

A side chair with the small fruits worked in petit point. *Courtesy, Mr. Jay Clark IV, worked by his mother, Mrs. Ida-Hays McCormick Wende; photo, Lee Salsbery.*

BIBLIOGRAPHY

Carrol, Alice, *The Good Housekeeping Needlecraft Encyclopedia* New York, Rinehart, 1947

Dean Beryl, *Ecclesiastical Embroidery*, London, B. T. Batsford, Ltd., 1958

de Dillmont, Therese, *Encyclopedia of Needlework*, France, D.M.C. Library

Gibbon, M. A., *Canvas Work*, London, G. Bell and Sons, Ltd., 1965

Hope, Mrs. George Curling, *My Working Friend*, London, W. H. Collingridge, circa 1850

Hughes, Therle, *English Domestic Needlework*, New York, Macmillan, 1961

Lent, D. Geneva, *Needlepoint as a Hobby*, New York, Harpers, 1942

Lewis, Griselda, (editor) *Handbook of Crafts*, London, E. Hulton & Company, Ltd., 1960

Picken, Mary Brooks; White, Doris, *Needlepoint Made Easy*, New York, Harpers, 1955

Snook, Barbara, *Needlework Stitches*, New York, Crown Publishers, 1963

Spears, Ruth Wyeth, *The Work Basket Embroidery Book*, New York, M. Barrows, 1941

Thesiger, Ernest, *Adventures in Embroidery*, New York, Studio Books, 1941

A Chippendale child's chair, only 10 inches across the back and 11 inches on the other sides; the heads of some of the animals are in petit point. *Courtesy, Mrs. Thomas P. Dillon, worked by her mother, Mrs. Edith Pratt Maxwell; photo, Lee Salsbery.*

INDEX

Algerian Eye Stitch   120
Alternating Stitch   91
Aubusson Stitch   52

Bargello Stitch   92
Basket Weave   48
Bazar Stitch   78
Bias Tent Stitch   48
Binding Stitch   137
Brick Stitch   91
Byzantine Stitch   111

Cashmere Stitch   109
Cashmere Stitch Worked Diagonally   110
Chain Stitch   133
Check Stitch   72
Checker Stitch   112
Closed Cat Stitch   66
Closed Herringbone Stitch   79
Continental Stitch   47
Cross Stitch   53
Cross Stitch Tramé   54
Crossed Corners Stitch   51

Darning Stitch   128
Diagonal Stitch   48, 114
Diagonal Florentine Stitch   108
Diagonal French Stitch   73
Diagonal Knit Stitch   106
Diagonal Long Armed Cross Stitch   65
Diagonal Shell Stitch   86
Diamond Eyelet Stitch   122
Double Stitch   60
Double Cross Stitch   59
Double Leviathan Stitch   63
Double Straight Cross Stitch   62

Encroaching Gobelin Stitch   102
Encroaching Oblique Stitch   103
Enlarged Parisian Embroidery   99
Eye Stitch   120

Fancy Cross Stitch   70
Fern Stitch   80
Fishbone Stitch   81
Flame Stitch   92
Florentine Stitch   92
Flower Stitch   126
French Stitch   84

German Stitch   107
Gobelin Stitch   88
Gobelin Tramé   90
Greek Stitch   64

Half Cross Stitch   46, 51
Herringbone Stitch   74
Herringbone Stitch Gone Wrong   75
Hungarian Embroidery Stitch   98

Interlocking Gobelin Stitch   102
Irish Stitch   96

Jacquard Stitch   111
Janina Stitch   87

Kalem Stitch   105
Knit Stitch   105
Knitting Stitch   105
Knotted Stitch   83

Laced Chain Stitch   134
Leaf Stitch   116
Long and Short Oblique Stitch   81
Long Armed Cross Stitch   64
Long Cross Stitch   67
Long Oblique with Running Stitch   118

Milanese Stitch   115
Moorish Stitch   114
Mosaic Stitch   107
Mosaic Stitch Done Diagonally   108

Oblique Slav Stitch   104
Oblong Cross Stitch   55
Oblong Cross Stitch with Back Stitch   56
Old Florentine Stitch   95
Oriental Stitch   115

Parisian Embroidery Stitch   97
Perspective Stitch   118
Plaited Stitch   74
Plaited Gobelin Stitch   77
Point de Tresse Stitch   82
Point Russe   112

Quick Point   51

Raised Work   132
Ray Stitch   120
Renaissance Stitch   88

Rep Stitch   52
Reverse Eyelet Stitch   123
Reverse Herringbone Stitch   75
Reverse Tent Stitch   105
Rice Stitch   61
Rococo Stitch   85
Roumanian Stitch   87
Running Cross Stitch   67

Scotch Stitch   112
Scotch Stitch Worked Diagonally   114
Six-color Herringbone Stitch   78
Slanting Gobelin Stitch   101
Smyrna Cross Stitch   58
Soumak Stitch   103
Star Stitch   120
Stem Stitch   118
Straight Gobelin Stitch   88
Surrey Stitch   131

Telescoped Herringbone Stitch   66
Tent Stitch   47
Tied Down Cross Stitch   68
Triangle Stitch   124
Triple Cross Stitch   71
Triple Leviathan Stitch   125
Turkey Work   129
Two-color Herringbone Stitch   76

Upright Cross Stitch   57
Upright Gobelin Stitch   88

Velvet Stitch   79

Web Stitch   127
Wicker Stitch   100
William and Mary Stitch   61
Woven Cross Stitch   69
Woven Cross Stitch Square   69

174   NEEDLEPOINT